C000132467

The Truth About Prison

Prisoners, Professionals and Families Speak Out

LAPWING
BOOKS

Richard W Hardwick

Published 2017 by Lapwing Books

Lapwing Books, 31 Southward

Northumberland NE26 4DQ

Copyright © Richard W Hardwick 2017

The right of Richard W Hardwick to be identified as the author of this work has been asserted by him in accordance with the Copyright, Designs and Patents Act 1988

All rights reserved. No part of this publication may be reproduced, stored in or introduced into a retrieval system, or transmitted, in any form, or by any means (electronic, mechanical, photocopying, recording or otherwise) without the prior permission of the publisher

A catalogue reference for this book is available from the British Library

Front cover photograph by George Hodan

ISBN 978-0-9569555-8-6

Printed by CreateSpace

Introduction

Richard W Hardwick

If you ask people who've just left prison about their experiences of being inside, their responses are fascinating and often quite frightening. If you ask professionals - such as prison officers, governors, probation officers, psychologists and teachers - to talk truthfully about their work within prisons and the criminal justice system, and you guarantee them anonymity, their responses are also fascinating, but highly revealing too. And when you read these stories together, you notice threads and themes that not only tell stories of personal redemption and endurance, of fear and violence, but of an insular environment that hides many of its challenges and secrets from the public. Professionals are not allowed to speak to the press and would be disciplined or sacked for doing so. There are valid reasons for this and the taxpaying public should know the truth.

Newspapers, computers and televisions bring us statistics and stories on an almost weekly basis: prisoners off their heads on drink and drugs; self-harm and suicide rates rising to a record high; an understaffed and underfunded prison service; a specialist team of counterterrorism experts aimed at tackling extremism; mindless violence captured on contraband mobile phones; inmates taking over whole wings through rioting.

I've travelled throughout England and Wales: from the South coast to Northumberland; from the mountains of Wales to an exposed beach by a raging North Sea. Participants were met in a place of their own choosing, whether that be their own home, a cafe or a particular walk they wished to do. My intention was to facilitate the right climate for participants to feel able to speak honestly. Having worked in numerous prisons for more than eight years, teaching creative writing, facilitating other creative projects and running prison magazines, I knew there was a need for this book. It's important to note, however, that my own opinions are not involved here. Yes, all questions are directive to some extent, but I did not direct interviewees towards any pre-determined assumptions or opinions, and the editing process has been ethical and truthfully represents each person. I've been stood up by a number of ex-prisoners, the most frustrating being a four-hour drive, confirmed the night before, to meet someone who wasn't in and then hung up on me. I guess this goes with the territory. Professionals agreed to meet and then changed their minds, either through ill-health or fear of being outed. I understand and respect these decisions.

How has government policy impacted upon all those affected? Are criminals leaving as better people, less likely to commit crime? What's the difference between high security, local and young offender prisons? Hundreds of terrorists have been imprisoned in the past decade - what affect does this have upon the prison population? Are psychologists, probation officers and teachers helping rehabilitate vulnerable and volatile criminals or simply ticking boxes? What is the effect on mothers, daughters and other family members when their loved ones are incarcerated? Do prisons actually work? And what kind of future are we heading towards? There are numerous books about prison already, but they are written from a single point of view. *The Truth About Prison* allows many to tell their stories, with the understanding that truth is relative and individual, and that opposing truths can both be valid. A book like this truly reveals what prisons are like for those that live and work in them.

Richard W Hardwick

Foreword

Professor Maggie O'Neill

The Truth About Prison shares the experiences and narratives of seven prisoners and three family members, alongside professionals who worked or are working in prisons – two prison officers, a governor, three prison teachers, three probation officers and a professor of Psychology. A brave book and a compelling read, it shares first-hand stories of criminal life, with inside accounts of life in youth offending institutions, male, female and high security prisons. These powerful but divergent accounts are critical to Hardwick's aim; to challenge the mythology and stereotypes about life inside the prison estate, and to share the utter complexity and multiple stories from those inside, the prisoners, their families and prison/probation staff.

The impact of managerialism and funding cuts on the quality of re-habilitation versus warehousing is defined very aptly in 'Capitalism's Elastoplast' and 'Benchmarked.' We are shown the backgrounds and contexts to the lives of those imprisoned, the impact of abuse, domestic violence, hegemonic masculinities and racism and the families left behind. Damage rather than rehabilitation is revealed, connected in part to poor governance and cuts in funding that mean risky levels of staffing, especially when dealing with bullying, violence, gang membership, drugs, self-harming and the tatters remaining of the safety net of care and support offered both inside and 'through the gate.' The section 'Have People Got A Heart?' should be essential reading for Social Work, Probation and Prison Officer training; indeed, this whole book should be. I will be using this text on my reading lists with BA Criminology and BA Sociology/Criminology students, alongside Pat Carlen's *Criminal Women,* John Podmore's *Out of Sight, Out of Mind: Why Britain's Prisons are Failing*, David Honeywell's *Never Ending Circles* and Erwin James' *A Life Inside: A Prisoner's Notebook.*

This is the third book written by Richard W Hardwick that attends to the life stories and social issues underpinning routes into (and out of) offending. In a sense, it is the obvious third part of what could be described as a trilogy. The first, *Kicked Out*, is described as a novel about today's unwanted youth, based on his experience of working with young people who offend and are homeless. The second, *Shattered Images and Building Bridges*, a powerful and beautifully illustrated book, is a collection of prisoners writing and artwork from three prisons where Richard worked as a creative writing tutor, giving voice to the vital importance of creativity, the space to write and its potential for changing lives.

And now, in *The Truth About Prison*, Richard looks at the prison system and attendant professions through the eyes, experiences and narratives of those closest to it. A complex, troubling and politically charged story unfolds and crucially, as Keith, the governor, states, "the strive towards managerialism loses sight of the fact that we're in a people business ... prisons are part of the community. We've got to ensure people in the community can see what is going on inside them." Richard's book responds to this and gives readers an insight into prisons, the socio-political contexts, governance, management, sentence planning, the shift to private prisons, the pressures on prison staff, the importance of prison education, the lived experiences, and the brutality alongside the small acts of kindness.

Professor Maggie O'Neill, Programme Director, BA Criminology and BA Sociology with Criminology, University of York

The Truth About Prison

Prisoners, Professionals and Families Speak Out

Contents

The Cast

Craig - sentenced to fourteen years, resident of three HMP prisons, two local and one high security

Val - sentenced to eleven years, resident of two HMP prisons, one closed and one open

Daniel - resident of numerous prisons over twenty-one years, HMP and private, local and high security

Colin - sentenced to ten years, resident at two high security prisons

Antonio - sentenced to twenty-five years, resident at two high security prisons

Billy - sentenced to five months in a Young Offenders Institute, and twelve months in an HMP adult prison

Paige - sentenced to three months in an HMP prison

Peter - Probation Officer for almost thirty years, currently writing sentencing reports at Crown Court

Donna - Probation Officer, working in field teams for more than twenty years

Caroline - Probation Service Officer, working in field teams and approved premises for five years, now working alongside Probation

John - Prison Officer at a local HMP prison for more than twenty years

Sarah - Prison Officer at a private prison for more than twenty years

Keith - Governor at numerous prisons for more than thirty years, including Number One Governor at male and female establishments

Stephen - Professor of Psychology for over twenty years, specialising in prisons

Adele - teacher at local HMP male and female prisons for more than ten years

Alice - teacher at a male high security prison for more than twelve years

Nigel - teacher at a female prison and a male high security prison for six years

Rebecca - mother of three boys, all imprisoned

Gary - father of a twenty-six year old man, three years into an eight year sentence

Sophie - nineteen year old girl, with a father in and out of prison throughout her life

Down to the Prison

Craig

The green outskirts of a northern industrial town. We walk by a field of buttercups, past dog walkers that nod heads and towards sycamore trees that rise at evenly spaced angles. Craig's been out nine months, having spent eight years inside the vulnerable prisoner wings at two local prisons and one high security prison. Olive skinned and bald headed, thick set and with a cheery face, he looks at the sycamores and smiles.

I planted these trees, every one of them. I know it's daft but it's a good legacy. It's what, thirty years on? I was happy back then, working for the council. I wished I'd stayed at it. They were two inch diameter, six foot saplings when I planted them, just spindly things. Now look at them.

The sharp sing-song of blackbirds and the constant chatter of swallows. I ask Craig about imprisonment, but he retreats further back to the day of his arrest.

I was in bed asleep and there was a shaking on me shoulders. I thought I was getting mugged, I didn't realise it was the police. They took us downstairs, told us what the charges were, then it was in the back of the van and down the station. It was Christmas Eve and I was due to see me daughter the next morning, but they took everything for forensics, even me shoes, so the next day I had Christmas clothes on with a pair of working boots. I lied to me ex-wife, said I'd been in a fight and lost one of me shoes. And from then on, I was living life but already serving me sentence, because I knew I was going to court and the chances were I'd be found guilty and go to prison, and I wasn't due in court until the following November. I had eleven months of it, going to the police station every week to sign in, wondering if they'd keep us 'til the trial. Every time I was talking to somebody, I thought it might be the last time. Every time I saw a police car, I thought it was for me. Every time the phone rang.

Val

Tall and lean, with long black hair, wearing a waterproof jacket and Converse trainers. We shake hands and walk out of the village. I check my map while Val, released from prison in 2015 having served five and a half years, picks her little dog up at the sound of a car engine.

He used to drink twenty-two pints a day, and I knew, I had this horrible feeling in my stomach when he was on his way home. I was suffering extreme domestic violence, I'd been nearly killed three times, so I decided to get revenge. I turned to the Yardies for protection, and whatever him and his family did to me in the day, I did back to them on the night. I took drugs to stay awake and I became feral. My daughters were seven, thirteen and eighteen when I was locked up. The little one was in nappies until she was nine because of what they done, like sneaking in our house in the night and holding a knife to my throat. I had scars all over my face from when they ran me over. They got me in this garden and beat me up, about forty of them. I drove my van through their front door. Every car they got, I smashed it up. I got one of them with a hammer. I came back one day and one of the lads had burnt all the stuff in my front room, smashed every window in my house and injected in my kitchen. I caught him and punched fuck out of him. His family tortured people, even this woman who had cancer and her disabled son, they shit all over her house. I was even more of a target because I was sticking up for her. So when I went to prison, it was fuck all, it was sanctuary.

Craig

I turned up for sentencing with a hidden Stanley blade, thinking, if I get found guilty, I'll slit me wrists. But they told us I'd get a Community Rehabilitation Order, so I opened me phone and the blade was behind the battery. Then a previous crime came up and I was re-arrested, and I didn't tell nobody because I was that ashamed, and I thought, if I don't get jail, nobody else will be none the wiser. When me girlfriend went to work, I put court clothes on and went to court. It got adjourned for mental health reports, other reasons. I went back home, got changed again and met her from work. She said, what have you been doing? I said, just pottering about. I did want support, but I was too ashamed, and I knew I was getting a guilty verdict now, despite what me solicitor said. I went behind the glass and seen this big screw and thought he hasn't been there all week. Everyone was doing something and wouldn't look at us. I heard handcuffs in the back getting sorted. The judge came in and did the summing up, but I was self-harming, constantly scratching the skin so I didn't have to listen. But I heard the word guilty, and it was like someone had punched us in the face, I couldn't breathe. Me solicitor suggested I play mentally ill. You'll go to a mental institution instead, he said, but once you feel better you'll go to prison and start your sentence. I was tempted, and thought I might as well be somewhere like that if I'm gonna end me life, but part of us knew I wouldn't be able to do that, because you never know, you might get a short sentence, and so even then you're in denial. They put handcuffs on and put us in the van. Other lads were shouting, asking what I'd been done for, but I didn't say a word, I was like a scared animal. I stood up and looked out the window, it was plastic and all scratched, and I went past the shops I knew, past the pubs I knew, and down to the prison.

Val

I told the judge I couldn't give a fuck. I'd never been to court before and I was exhausted and covered in scars. I sat in the park that morning, thinking, just when I've found peace, I'm going away. I was drinking at the time to numb everything. They'd got my daughter and put gloss paint all over her hair. They'd done all sorts to us. They tried to burn my house down and we were moved out the area, but we sneaked back at night-time just to say it was home, because we were sleeping in

14

the park at the time. I told the kids, I'm going to jail, but I want you to know that I love you. Things have to be the way they are, you have to be big and strong. There was loads of our friends in the gallery, but when I told the judge I couldn't give a fuck, he cleared the gallery and gave me another five years, so I got eleven instead of six. In my mitigation, the coppers had been called out to my address about two hundred times, but then I got a crossbow and said, if you don't do anything about this, I'm going to shoot anyone who comes through the door, because my kids are terrified.

Billy

Medium height, with a fighter's build and tattoo-covered arms and hands; Billy invites me into his home and moves baby toys and playthings so I can sit on the couch. His girlfriend smiles and goes to make me a cup of tea, their baby under her arm. The telly is on; In The Night Garden with Igglepiggle, Upsy Daisy and Makka Pakka. Billy watches the programme as he talks to me.

I was brought up to be violent. When I was five, this young lass was playing with something I wanted so I smashed a brick off her head. That was the way I was brought up. Violence was bred into me. When I was ten, there was this older lad in the street who'd done something to me, and my dad, who was in our house drinking with his friends, gave me this pick-axe handle and said, if you don't bray him with it, then I'm going to bray you with it. So, for my dad and his friends pleasure, I went out and brayed this kid. And that was normal.

Daniel

A new estate, strategically placed a few miles from the main A road that serves the region. Daniel answers the door, wearing a t-shirt that moulds around tattoo-covered muscles. He's arranged to meet me at his father's house, as it grants him another reason to pay a visit. I accept a cup of tea and partake in polite chatter, but Daniel's father, a successful and legitimate businessman, looks uncomfortable when the conversation slips into his son's past. And so we decide to go for a drive instead and sit inside Daniel's BMW. He admits he has no idea where he is; he's only been here once before and he followed the Sat Nav. Don't worry I say, just drive.

The first time I got locked up was in 1995, so I was fifteen. I'd been remanded into the care of the local authority because I got done for nicking a motorbike and my mum wouldn't have me back. I met other kids in trouble and did street robberies, and from the age of sixteen to twenty-two, I was never out of jail more than three months. I wanted to be this notorious guy with a fearsome reputation, because when you grow up in these kids homes, that's all people live on. I wanted to be the biggest baddest fucker in the whole area. And so I learned from everybody I met, I absorbed everything, every crime somebody had done. I'd say, what are you in for? How did you get caught? I'd listen and think right, I'll not get caught that way. I watched Police, Camera, Action to see what they were looking for. Then I turned twenty-one and ended up in adult prison. Altogether, I've been in six adult prisons, two privatised and one high security. I've been out just over a year now and I'm thirty-six, so I've been twenty one years in and out of all types of prisons.

Billy

I was always trying to impress my dad. I was his party piece. He used to force me to be violent to others and then gloat about it. But actually my mam was more violent towards me and my brother, she dished out more of the beatings. She hit me more than forty times with a belt once. I had welts all over my back and had to stay off school so nobody knew. Social Services were never called because we moved house that often, and neighbours put up petitions to get us evicted. Our whole family was violent and my mam and dad were always on drink and drugs. Everywhere we moved, something happened.

Colin

With a chiselled face, sharp stubble and piercing eyes, Colin has a cinematic presence that suggests numerous journeys throughout his forty-six years. He shakes my hand and I notice his fingers are tattooed with pagan symbols. Over Victorian architecture and shabby industrial estates on a seventies flyover we drive, and then out of town, past fields of crops and cattle. I don't ask about the GPS tag fitted onto his ankle, but I know it's there because he told me about it during our phone call. Then he begins talking about prison, and I wonder if someone is tracking us on a computer.

I was whisked away by unmarked cars, taken to a secure police station and intensely questioned without anybody knowing where I was. If you created levels of questioning where shoplifting was one and murder was ten, then mine was around fifteen. I didn't get any sleep, they questioned me day and night, the psychiatrist stopped it because I wasn't in a fit state to continue. I had no conception of time but I was told afterwards it was two weeks. The law says you can only be held for a day or two, so they kept putting a video camera in front of me and the judge gave them more time. Then I was rushed to a secure remand unit inside a prison, where I was on remand and in isolation, apart from suited and booted prison guards, for almost a year. It was hell on earth. I had to put an application in for exercise every morning, then I'd be marched down to this small yard. They often forgot about me, so I spent an hour wanting to be back in again. The only other time out of my cell was for a shower, and I had to apply for them each morning as well. Other than that, I spent all the time in my cell, because I wasn't being questioned, they'd finished that at the police station. Then they told me I was moving and bundled me into a paddy wagon, just me and five screws. I was double-cuffed by large padlocks with a small chain between, and when I went off the van I was cuffed to a screw. They made me wear a banana suit, a yellow and green boiler suit, but I was so desperate to get out that unit I'd have gone anywhere, I'd have gone to Guantanamo Bay if they'd asked me.

Antonio

We pick our way around the corner of an imposing rock face; Antonio, his wife Layla and I, all inappropriately dressed and shivering. Layla's wearing heels and a mock fur coat. Antonio, a thick set man in his late forties, is wearing a black jacket and black trousers. Ten minutes later, the great mountain stands colossal in front of us, its snow covered peak catching glimpses of sunlight that have slipped through dense cloud. Off the path we step, carefully, to rest our backsides on a huge cold boulder and wait for Antonio to light his cannabis joint in the breeze.

When I was young, I used to fight the screws, and so I was always down the block and I lost all my remission. But this time I was thirty-eight and in this high security remand unit where they have thirteen prisoners and fifteen staff, so by circumstance you're forced to associate with screws. They're all really amicable. Don't call me sir, don't call me boss, I'm Pete, I'm a good lad me. And they are very amicable lads, no doubt, but they're all very big lads as well. I was watching rugby on a rare association period and one of them sat down on the couch. He said he'd been in the normal prison. I've had this right big argument with some fucking black kid, he said, and he was proper cunting me off. I was wondering what he was gonna do, because a screw who nicks someone is a dog, but a screw who never nicks anyone is alright. And so I asked him, and he went, nah, you know me mate, I wouldn't do that. But listen to what he said next, because this set me up for the rest of my sentence. He said, if he thinks he's getting away with treating me like that though, I'll phone a mate who works in census and every one of his fucking letters are going missing now. He thinks he's getting his visiting orders? There'll be sudden glitches. Then I'll phone my mate in finance and all his money he's getting sent in, his canteen for tobacco, his toiletries, there's gonna be glitches with that as well. And another of my mates works with dogs on reception, so any visitors that do come, the dog's gonna knock on them, so they'll have to have a closed visit or fuck off. And inside, from the neck down, I went cold as ice, not with anger, but with fear, because I was just starting a twenty-five year sentence, and I wanted to fight these fuckers, that was my mental state. I thought, I'll never get out, I've got over twelve years remission to lose, I've got to play this different. I remembered when I was a kid and I tried to get in this illegal blues den in the black area of the city, and the doormen told me to fuck off or I'd get a slap. But I wouldn't, I'd back off, stay longer and say, they're smart trainers them mate. And if anyone kicked off, I'd get involved and help them. In the end they'd say, just get yourself in you little twat. And that was how I decided to deal with the screws. If I heard someone say, alright George, next time I saw that screw I'd say the same, and I know he's read my shit in the paper, and he thinks it's mint some fucking gangster knows he's called George.

Billy

I was getting sentenced for Actual Bodily Harm, Aggravated TWOC (Taking a Vehicle Without the Owner's Consent), Driving Without Licence and Insurance, Criminal Damage, and some Drunk and Disorderlies. I'd gone off the rails basically, but I was eighteen and thought there was a good chance I'd get off. I didn't even understand how many crimes I was up for and I was really hungover. The judge called me back in and these two big Group 4 Security blokes walked in and I thought, oh dear. They cuffed me to them and the judge spouted all this stuff. I had to ask how long I was going to prison for. He said five months and I got took away and put in a holding cell. You see all these programmes and hear all these stories and I was really nervous.

Paige

Every knock on Paige's door is louder than the previous one. I'm beginning to think she's hiding inside and has changed her mind about talking to me. I wonder if I should put my face to the living room window instead; I can hear children's programmes on the television. But then she arrives behind me, having dropped her children off at pre-school for the afternoon. We go inside and sit on her couch, and stay there the whole time, in the same positions, as she scratches her wrist and answers my questions nervously and quietly.

I was shitting myself because I knew I was going to jail. I had nine Actual Bodily Harm's and one Grevious Bodily Harm on my record, and I'd been to a Secure Training Centre and been warned if anything else happened I would go to jail. But my mam passed away and I went off the rails. I set a fight up with all these gypsies and got grassed up. I was sentenced to three months but I only did eight weeks because I did good and didn't kick off or anything, so I got released on a tag.

Craig

We drove through massive gates, two of them. They took us out and asked us loads of questions, put us in a cubicle and didn't shut the curtain. I had to take all me clothes off and turn around, and I heard people laughing and thought they were laughing at me. It's just a normal work environment for them, but it was the most painful and degrading thing in my life. Then I was allowed a phone call, so I rang mam. She said, hiya son, where are you? I said, mam, I'm in jail, and I had to tell her what for. And I knew she was gonna read the papers and there was nothing I could do, and I wished I'd had time to say this might happen, that might happen, or tell me brothers, mam's gonna need you. Because of self-harming, they put us on the hospital wing. I thought, at least I'm not going into the main prison, I'll have a hospital ward and it will be ideal. But it wasn't, it was a cell exactly the same as the others, but all I got was a concrete bed, a concrete table and a concrete stool. There wasn't a kettle, there wasn't a cup, I didn't have a blanket, there was absolutely nothing. I had two cameras looking at us and the light was on all night. It was the longest night of me life.

Val

They put me in a cell and nobody came near me for four weeks, Probation, screws, prisoners, nobody, because I was still feral and I'd have fucking killed them. I had nightmares and I slept with the light on.

Was there a time when you started trusting anyone?

I don't trust anyone, I'll never trust anyone. I took that to jail and it's done me good.

Billy

I went to Young Offenders in a sweatbox. All the lads were talking normally, saying how long they'd got and what for. When I told them I'd only got five months, they said, oh that's a shit and a shave that.

Craig

Next morning they opened the door. They didn't say, go and get your breakfast, they just opened the door. I put me head out all cautious like, is this a trick? I saw all these cons in their jeans and blue striped shirts and I followed them to the kitchen area and everybody was staring at us. I assumed they knew the worst, so from day one I was expecting to get battered. The only time it eased was when mental health chatted to us, because working with them in the past, I knew they were on my side. But whereas before, they could put us somewhere and get us help, in there they couldn't, and what I found was, the more I assured them I could be trusted, they would give us a kettle, teabags, toilet roll and bits and pieces. Eventually, they moved us onto the wing itself. They had Vulnerable Prisoner wings but I didn't know what VP was then, so fortunately, with me mental health, I had me own cell, because most had two or three people in. But that put us in a dilemma, because if I got better mental health wise, they'd put us in a shared cell and I'd go downhill again. And so I made it plain that if I was put with someone else I might lash out.

Daniel

Imagine the last year of school. You always get four or five lads bullying everybody. Then imagine a wing full of them, that's what young offenders is like. Everybody's out to create. Everybody wants to be top dog, it was absolute mayhem. And in 1995 there was no telly in your cell, no right to exercise every day, you got your meals and were locked up most the time. I had a pad mate because you got doubled up. We played table tennis. We used the ball out a roll-on deodorant, had two bits of mirror as bats and took a line out the sheet as a net. We bullied people out the door when anyone new came in, we shouted at them for something to do. If you got enhanced, you were allowed a radio, so you had your favourite programmes, like the top 40 on a Sunday. You got yourself into a regime and it became the norm, and after a while I kind of liked it, because when I first went in I was fifteen and everyone bullied me, but then I got to the eighteen mark and I was top of the food chain. From there, you go into an adult jail and you've gone from being the big I am to this young kid, and when you get bullied it's more serious because they're grown blokes. But at that point in my life, I honestly didn't give a fuck, I was constantly fighting. If anyone said anything, I'd unleash on them straight away, and it got to the point where people left me alone. So once again, that fed my ego. I was a twenty-one year old knocking thirty-year olds out. And being in an adult prison, feeling that respect and power, you take that back out onto the street.

Billy

The first couple of weeks were hard. I didn't know what to say, what to do or where to go. They offered me this horrible microwave meal in reception that I wouldn't feed to the dog. I gave it to the other lads, a big regret because I was starving later. I got my bedsheets, my grey clothes. I got checked over by the nurse. Nobody explained anything to me. And then I sat in my cell, looked out this horrible window onto massive wire fences and thought, what the fuck.

Colin

I was plastered all over the media well before I was convicted. When it got to court, there was no point going to trial, because it was already a done deal. I was told if I pleaded not guilty and was found guilty I'd get seven years Imprisonment for Public Protection, which would be a life sentence really. If I pleaded guilty I'd get ten years, so I thought that was my best option, and I don't think guilt or innocence came into that, it was about self-preservation. IPP prisoners always do a lot more than their sentences stipulate. They've abolished it now for that reason, but they haven't done anything about those still serving them. I met one lad who had an eighteen month IPP and he was still in prison seven years later, it was horrendous. And it's impossible to prove you're not a risk to the public.

Paige

I went in one of those paddy wagons and there was a paedophile next to me. He got dropped off at the male prison, then we went to the women's and the guards pushed me out the van. They made me do wee samples to see if I was on drugs, but I was only on green, cannabis.

Craig

Mental health listened and I kept that cell to meself. But people kept coming to the door and asking what I was in for, so I hid under the bed, thinking if they looked through the flap, they'd think I was out. I put the chair there, the table with a towel over, and I laid under the bed and watched telly on the other side of the room and ignored people banging on the door. They banged twice as much though, because they realised someone was in there hiding, they saw weakness and pounced on it. But bit by bit, I got out. In the meds queue, I talked to the person in front because the person behind was having a go about what I'd done. I went to the library and talked to people there. Then I got me first canteen sheet and it said I had £1.15 and I didn't have any clue you got money in jail, so I bought a pencil and a bag of sweets. And when a letter came, I used the envelope and drew a caravan on it. I drew me freedom, and it was only a childish picture but it gave us hope.

Daniel

And then you go from adult prison into high security and it's a total different kettle of fish. In Cat B, I bullied people but I never got caught for anything, so in the prison officer's mind I was a really good prisoner. The officers made me head of the cleaners and I kept order on the wing. I didn't like people kicking the doors at night, I wanted to sleep. I didn't like them pressing the bells unless it were an emergency because it woke everybody up. I like the wing clean because I'm that type of person, and I don't know how many times I beat the fucking shower cleaner up because the showers weren't clean. Then they said, you're going to Rye Hill. I got on the bus and the governor said, you're not going to Rye Hill, you're going to high security. He waited until I was locked in the bus because I would have kicked off. So I got to this high security prison and I'd heard all these stories and I was completely on edge, because every time you go to a new prison, you're wondering what's behind the gate and what's going to happen to you.

Antonio

The first five years I was claustrophobic and desperate to get on the landing, even if I hated the wankers that were on the wing, even if I detested every screw. All those moments you're in a cell, if a flood or an earthquake came, if your kids are dying, you're not getting out, no matter what, it's a fucking steel box. The landings in high security are all pretty much the same; groups of blokes, loads of testosterone and sweat, uncontrolled emotions and people with irrational thinking and social skills, just fucking crazy basically. Everything from extreme terrorists hugging people but stabbing them in the back to murderers. Every type of crime you can commit, and nearly all violent. After the first five years though, depending on the landing, it was get me behind my fucking door, not because of any fear or sense of danger, but because they're fucking idiots. There's people who'll just walk into your cell and say, morning mate, then nick a roll-up when you're in the shower. And I'm not bothered about them nicking a roll-up, but this type of person wouldn't have my number outside, I wouldn't introduce them to my mother, if I knew who she was, I wouldn't let my kids shake their hands. He might have killed a granny. Actually, he wouldn't have killed a granny because he wouldn't be in my fucking cell, but he might have killed his best mate over a bag of heroin, you know, something fucking horrible. So yeah, the second seven years or so, you're dying to get back in your cell, unless you're doing something constructive like gym or education.

And what did you make of your cell?

Well any traumatic experience in life brings out any suppressed fucking mentalist stuff you've got going on, and a lot of lads with big sentences turn OCD on themselves. They get curtains and carpets, it looks like a fucking lounge, you've got to take your shoes off when you go in. That was not my fucking home, it was their fucking kennel. I tipped cigarettes on the floor and brushed dust underneath my bed, it was a fucking dump. All I kept clean was my bog and sink. Some of the OCD lads came and blitzed my cell for me. Fuck that, I wanted to never forget I was in prison.

Craig

Eight months I was in there and I never shaved once. Me beard must have been seven inches and it was pure grey, me hair had grown back and was itching like hell and I was still scratching meself, so I was constantly getting wrapped up. Then someone from high security came and said they could help but I needed to stop self-harming and clean meself up. So the next day I got the courage to go down to the barber. He shaved the top off first and left the beard, and people were going by saying, fuck me, it's Charles Bronson, and that made us giggle, for the first time in eight months. And then I got talking to different people and built me confidence a little, and went out on the exercise yard, just sitting near the screws at first, but eventually going for a couple of laps. Then they sent us to high security. I'd heard stories about how awful it was, how certain people were in there, and I was never a Category A prisoner, I was Category B, but when I got there it was better than the local. I had me own cell, they had more education and work, you got better money so you had better canteen, and I was on the VP wings so I didn't have to worry as much about getting battered. Then it came to sentencing and a taxi picked us up, me and two screws. The driver didn't know where Crown Court was, so it was me telling him where to go, with the screws laughing like hell. And I still didn't know the sentence because I totally zoned out, I just looked at the piece of wood on the dock and nothing went in, it was like white noise. A couple of days later I realised I had eight years, so it was a case of buckling down and doing the best I could.

Val

I loved jail. I loved the safety and security of it. The only thing that was hard was not having my kids. I asked the dad, look after Tina, but he said no. The youngest two ended up on the estate I'd come from, where all the shit happened. I'd told social workers I didn't want my kids going there. This guy came to my house with a machete and the little one hid behind the sofa, but they still put her with his family because domestic violence is accepted there, it's seen as the norm, and the social workers didn't realise how bad the family were. I thought about my girls all the time, it tortured me. The little one was such a baby, she was going through pure hell and couldn't say anything because she knew there'd be consequences. The middle one was raped and held hostage. They came to see me three times in the first year and it was amazing, I couldn't believe how much they'd grown. But then the family put them against me, so they never came anymore.

Daniel

We pulled up and parked at an angle so I could see this high security jail, and I thought fuck, this looks like a serious place. We got through the gate and four officers with shields, all kitted up, came onto the bus. I'd never seen prison officers with dogs before, drug dogs yes, but not Alsatians. They said, are you coming in quietly or are we pulling you in? I said, no I'm alright me, I'll come quietly. I walked into reception and they said, you've never been in high security before, we'll give you a tip. If you go onto the wing and anybody's got a problem with you, just hide in your cell, don't stand and fight because these lads will kill you. I walked up this concrete runway all the way to F-Wing and the prison's on exercise, so there's a yard to my left, a yard to my right, and everyone's staring at me. I got onto the wing and I could tell it wasn't like any other jail I'd been in before. There was hardly any noise and there seemed more officers than prisoners. I looked around and thought fuck, everyone looks massive. And when you're talking to people in high security, you can see in their eyes they're totally different to any other prisoner. I don't know what it is, but the stories they tell you, you think fucking hell.

Billy

I was in one young offenders for four or five weeks, then another for four months. Then I got out and had a lucky string of not getting caught for violence until I was nineteen and got sent down again. I was on remand for two months and got sentenced to twelve more, and this was in an adult prison because they'd closed the young offenders. Adult prison was horrible. It seemed chilled out but the consequences were more serious. Young offenders, you could have a straightener in the shower. In adult prison you were locked up with some nasty bastards.

Paige

I got kicked out in Year 6 because I smacked a teacher. Then I went to another school but I was only in there two weeks and then I got kicked out of there for calling the Head Teacher and smashing his window. The next school I was in there for two years, but then I hit a support teacher and never went back. Then they put me in a Secure Training Centre and it was a piece of piss. Things kicked off nearly every day, especially with lasses. But you get PlayStations, takeaways and everything. You're allowed to mix with the boys and you can order Avon products if you have enough money. It was like a giant youth club or holiday camp, I loved it. My mam was alive then, she came to see me three times a week. Maybe if I'd learned my lesson there I wouldn't have got sent down. But then I got out after three months and six months later my mam passed away.

Val

There was this lass, she got done for chucking rhubarb at her brother's car, but the fucking car crashed straight into a tree and killed him. I couldn't stop laughing when she told me, she looked like a schoolteacher. There were nurses in there, doctors, all kinds, really intelligent people. And this other lass, she was beautiful, but she walked around with this dazed expression on her face. You should never ask a lifer what they're in for, but I did, I was intrigued. She'd had a baby, it was only six weeks old, and her husband came back and started on her because he'd been drinking, so she picked a knife up, stabbed him and killed him. She had this sheer look of despair and wondering where she was the whole time.

Capitalism's Elastoplast

Peter

I started at Probation in the late eighties. I was working with people being decanted out of long-term mental health institutions into the community, but I was funding for my own job on a rolling four week contract, not an enviable position for a guy with a mortgage and two young children. The Probation Service I joined was very white, very middle aged, very middle class and very middle brow. People typically came in with life experience, in their mid-thirties, and the younger generation of qualified officers were bringing in notions of equality of opportunity and anti-discriminatory practice, what became disparagingly referred to as political correctness gone mad. But it was a very good and necessary thing, and most of the people who drew it to ridicule were the people who had the most compromised values.

Donna

When I was twelve I did voluntary work in a mother and baby rehabilitation unit. I've always cared for people who were struggling with life. I studied Social and Community Studies when I was seventeen, and in 1985, aged twenty five, I did a degree in Community and Social Work, with the intention of becoming a social worker. I did my last placement in Probation though, and it was a lot easier because you were more protected, you were an officer of the court, so you weren't going to get filled in like a social worker. I've spent the last eleven years doing purely resettlement, with a case load of prisoners serving twelve months or over and coming out on licence. I've been going into prisons for twenty odd years.

Caroline

I applied for the Diploma in Probation in 1999, did a year of my traineeship in the field team and had an horrendous year. My practice teacher had been married, had a son and was a perpetrator of domestic violence, then he left his marriage, came out as gay and lived with another guy. He made instant decisions about whether he liked people or not, and if he didn't like you there was no going back. He said, it's my business to make sure you don't pass. I'd do a piece of work for him, he'd rip it to bits, give me it back and say, that's sugar-coated shit, do it again, but not give advice on how to improve it. I had that a for a whole year, and honestly, he was representative of the training department. But one woman, seconded from Probation to University for the academic side of things, she was lovely and supportive. I'd refused to do an assignment and got the union involved because this guy was being destructive. You're on for a first, she said. Your academic work's fine, and I know what you're dealing with because he's a shit. I told her I was going to leave, I wasn't putting myself through it anymore. We'll give you a Probation Service Officer role, they said. We don't want to lose you, we've invested time and money and you've got skills we can use. So I went to another field team and loved it. The staff were fantastic and the manager was really supportive. The guy who'd been my practice teacher was taken out of training and became diversity manager, and it must have been because he was gay, because he was the most un-diverse person you could ever meet.

Stephen

I've worked in the mental health arena, in psychiatric hospitals, in women's prisons, high security prisons, training prisons and with young offenders. I've done direct one-to-one clinical work such as suicide prevention, group work such as anger management, and then at an organisational level, including how to select and train prison officers, and training psychologists. I've also worked in central government, influencing policy.

Peter

I've visited prisons many times, mainly for sentence planning and post course reviews. I come from the day when you visited prisoners, it was part of what you did. And the more you put into the person, face to face, pre-release, the better chance you have of a successfully completed licence period. Why wouldn't I respond better to you, if you took the trouble to come and see me? Because part of the job, especially with guys serving long times, you'll probably have to say things they don't want to hear, such as, you're not doing as well as you think you are, there are areas you need to go into that you're declining to acknowledge. One guy who'd disengaged for a long period, his rationale was, I'll behave as if I don't care whether I'm getting out or not, then they've got nothing to hold over me. He found the segregation unit suited him. From my point of view, this is a maladaptive coping strategy. From his point of view, you don't understand my reality, this means they can't break me. And perhaps there's a dimension of control in there, an attempt to control an environment in which you're supposed to be powerless.

Caroline

I loved the challenge of working with people on how to break their patterns of offending. The way Probation was set up then was very different to now. You had individual meeting rooms so you could work with somebody on a one-to-one basis. Now it's like American Diner, you're sitting back to back. How can you do one-to-one offence based work with fifteen other people seeing fifteen other offenders in the same room? It doesn't make sense.

Peter

Lord Denning was right when he said, justice delayed was justice denied. I accept that. But there's a world of difference between preventing self-indulgent delay, often because of lack of preparation within the Crown Prosecution Service, and a desire of offence lawyers to have more balls in the air than they can actually bat. There weren't drop down menus when I started, I had a biro, an ashtray and my own office. My first year, every report I wrote was gate kept by a team manager, every one, and we also gate kept each other's reports, so you learn a lot from your colleagues, both in terms of confidence in your own work, and from more experienced people that are particularly eloquent or descriptive. Personally, I think a well written pre-sentence report is a thing of pride. But let's talk about good stuff first. We're well trained, we're pretty well supervised, we're the best agency I'm aware of, and I would include Psychology but perhaps not Psychiatry, at risk assessment, and we're the best at risk management. We work alongside Public Protection Units and MAPPA (Multi-Agency Public Protection Arrangements), we're key players and we've earned our seat at the table. We're good at protecting children and we're good at managing dangerous guys.

Caroline

Risk assessments were paper based and hand-written. I loved them, but they were so bloody subjective. What I perceived as a risk, somebody else might not, and it doesn't matter how much training you give people, it's still open to interpretation. They tried to take out subjectivity and streamline things. They came up with this tool called OAYSIS and it was introduced with a massive launch and two day training course. It's all about getting everybody thinking and working the same they said. It's going to be seamless, start at the beginning of their sentence, go all the way through with them and come out the other end. And it was drop down menus, pick something from these options. It stripped away autonomy, and yes consistency is important, but it shouldn't dictate and it does. You can only pick what's there, and you're working with people that change constantly, their circumstances change constantly, and when you're trained in Probation, they drill into you that risk is dynamic, it alters with situations and circumstances. So why not make the bloody tool dynamic? Give staff a little bit of autonomy back, give them space to think, because you're training people to have opinions and then not allowing them to express them.

Peter

Delius is our new recording system, and people will tell you, depending on how far up the management food chain you go, what a great tool it is. I'm here to tell you, that like much of the IT in the public sector, if the people who designed it at great expense worked for Amazon, they'd be sacked. You can lose work in it. You can literally lose a parole report, the product of eight hours work. We have a drop down menu for pre-sentence reports, five hundred character limit in risk assessment, and three hundred character limit in response to previous supervision. Three hundred characters is six lines. I couldn't tell you their criminal history, some of them, in six lines. Now given what I said to you about our excellence in risk assessment, why on earth don't we let ourselves explore it? It's madness, absolute madness. This Delius is a matter of huge regret, known without affection as Delirious.

Caroline

It took years for prison and Probation to marry up, and for OASYS 2 to follow through. And I trusted a handwritten risk assessment far more than a computer print-out, because you knew someone had taken the time to actually think about that individual. But if you haven't the space to put individual opinion, then you know it's just a generic document, and staff shouldn't have to read between lines when looking at medium or high risk offenders. And when you're scared the tool isn't appropriate, you err on the side of caution, sometimes extreme caution, because God forbid you miss something and somebody goes out and commits a heinous offence, that you're accountable for. And so tools like OASYS become a back covering exercise, and that's not what Probation should be about, it should be about rehabilitation and working with offenders to address behaviour. But that's statutory services on the whole now, isn't it? Let's make sure we're safe and secure before we think about the people we're working with. It's a sad state of affairs.

Donna

The last report I did before I went on the sick for my heart operation, was for a lad who'd been involved in Affray and was going down. Nobody had actually done anything to help him. I put my heart operation back three weeks and did my report, my style, and the judge said, thank goodness, this is a real piece of work, an old fashioned report. And I was chuffed, but I've never done a report like that again. That report made a difference, and I personally think I've made a difference, but more and more of the job has been going where you can't. Things began to change about 2007, 2008, and it wasn't the officers fault; they were being told what mattered by assessments on computers and time constraints.

Peter

We don't break down into soundbites very easily, do we? We're complicated people with complex needs, a multifariously messed up community. I worked with a woman who was old-school. She used to say, we're capitalism's Elastoplast. And I don't know if that was true when she started in the seventies, but Thatcher made it true, didn't she? The message was clear; not only do we not want you, but actually we need you to be unwanted, because you provide a mechanism for human wages, for institutionalising and so on. And increasingly, there's a poverty of aspiration. A poet friend of mine working in a primary school asked the kids, what do you want to be, when you leave school? Five or six wanted to be famous, as an end in itself, a kind of X Factor effect, but this one girl wanted to be a checkout worker. My friend said, why do you want to do that? She said, that's what my mam does. He said, do you not want something different, perhaps more challenging? And she said, well, if I just want that, then I won't be disappointed. And by the time these kids come to us, they've been social-worked, and have a way of describing themselves and sometimes very real trauma in their families and lives that they've survived, that they give you their story like a hand of medium trumps.

A Hand of Medium Trumps

Daniel

The first night, I was tidying my cell and had my stereo on. The next morning, this old feller James walked in and said, if you ever have your music on again, while I'm watching EastEnders, I will fucking kill you. I spoke to somebody on the wing and he went, yeah, he's a fucking mad-head him, just ignore him and be careful. Two weeks later, he come back in my cell and said, was you playing Fleetwood Mac over dinner? I thought, oh shit, here we go again. But he said, can I borrow it? So I lent him it, and I never got it back, I never even asked for it back. But I started talking to him, and he was sentenced to natural life, he wasn't just a lifer. I was sat in his cell looking at pictures of his daughter, his family and dog, and I said to him, how do you live every day, knowing you will never get out? I couldn't do it. And he said, the reason you can't do it, is you haven't done anything to warrant it. I've killed six people, so I sit on my bed every night knowing I deserve to be here.

Val

My first time at canteen, these four lasses came up and said, go over there and give this fucking message, that when we see so and so we're going to kill them. I said, I don't think so, I don't do messages. And I'm glad I never, because the lass they were threatening hung herself the next day. See, you get a hierarchy, but I'm a gym freak and I lift weights, and I knocked around with the hardest lass in prison. So I had a good pecking order because they knew I wasn't frightened, I've had to stick up for myself all my life. I got this lass called Christina to do my sandwiches because the young offenders spat in them. I was on four Prozac a day and I wouldn't let anyone jump the meds queue. I'd tell them to move or I'd move them myself, and I could feel my mouth talking, but my mind was saying, what are you going to do? Anything could have happened. But once they knew I wasn't bothered what anyone said or thought of me, and that I'd fight back, they backed off. I wasn't hard, I just wouldn't back down.

Billy

Young offenders was violent. The second day I was there, someone launched a pool ball off someone's head, for nothing. I got put to the test pretty quick. This lad said, I'll play you at pool for a quarter of baccy. I don't smoke but I got a pack when I got in. I potted the black before it was all cleared up. He said, I win. I said, no, it's re-spot the black. We argued about it, but he was just this skinny little freak who'd mugged someone. Lots of people stopped and stared. I said, you want your fucking baccy, come and get it. He said, I'll see you in the shower. I said, get in the shower then. I saw him in another young offenders a few months later, we were in the same maths class. He said, you still owe me some baccy. He was showing off in front of others. I told him to fuck off and he never said much after that.

Paige

I had my own cell because I was seventeen. If you're eighteen you have to share, so it was good I had my own cell because I didn't want to be someone else's bitch. I didn't know anyone in there and I was literally shitting myself. And I wanted to do myself in because I had nothing to live for. But after three weeks I met a few people and they seemed alright so I stuck with them. I'm still in contact with one of them, she's in a psychiatric hospital now because she self-harmed that bad. It's high security isn't it? For nutters. Proper nutters. She's the only one I'm still in touch with.

Colin

After trial they took me to a high security prison. I'd been to prison before but that was young offenders. The first couple of weeks was settling in, learning the ropes, and it was a bit scary. Everybody's interested in who you are, what you've done and what you're about, and I'd been all over the papers and news, so people had heard of me. Main wings can be gang or clique orientated. Muslims, blacks and whites tend to stick together. Some of the Muslims tried to convert me, they gave me an English version of the Koran with sections underlined about fighting non-believers. They said Allah would forgive me and kept asking me into cells to discuss religion.

Were you tempted?

Not at all. I think I'm the type of person that does the complete opposite of what someone tells me, that's probably got me into trouble most my life. And I do appreciate discussions on society, but this wasn't discussion, it was convert or else. So I took the or else like I often do. People do convert in prison, but it's out of fear, I don't think they genuinely convert, they look to belong and have back-up and protection. And because I wouldn't convert the self-proclaimed wing imam put a hit on my life. A couple of guys came to stab me with shanks but were outnumbered so changed their mind. The prison found out about it and moved me down the block.

Daniel

High security was a wake-up call. You can cook your own meals and you get more freedom but in stricter conditions. In Cat B you're in your cell more, but you're allowed on the exercise yard more and you never get escorted to certain places. High security seemed to give you more freedom, but really you were never off the wing, unless you were going somewhere like education or gym. And the atmosphere was much more tense. I cleaned my cell every Friday, but in high security I was told, make sure you clean your cell from door to wall, keep your eyes on your door all the time. It got to the point where I washed my hair with my eyes open, because everything happened in the showers. See, because I wasn't in a certain religious group, I was an outcast to certain people, and because I believed in respecting the country, a lot of people found that offensive. And lots of lads carry weapons, so I made sure I never slipped up and was facing every door. When we trained in the gym, there were three of us, someone training, someone helping and someone keeping an eye out. We cooked in twos, one cooking and the other making sure everything was alright behind you. It was constant, all the time, so it became natural.

Craig

Getting behind me door, that was a big thing. I did that lots at first, but then I realised about going into the yard. The yard in high security has cells on all sides, it's just a square and you go round anti-clockwise for about an hour. I couldn't communicate with the young lads because they had this daft sense of bravado, and to feel better about themselves, they'd look for somebody with a worse crime and tell everyone. I walked with older lads. They had something interesting to say about past lives, or we had something in common like farming and gardening. But sometimes I took sugar sachets with us and every time I got to a certain point, I took a slug of sugar. When I got to thirty laps I'd think I done well there. Some of that was to keep fit or pass the time, but sometimes you just need your own space, and if you walk slowly, somebody will come for a chat. I'd been in education all day, I've had to talk to screws, teachers, be pleasant to lads in class I don't get on with. I've come back, queued for dinner, queued for meds, queued for canteen, and until you get locked up, even if you go in your cell, the door's still open so people come in and out. So walking fast, people wouldn't come over. And if you got enhanced you could go onto A wing, which had a considerably bigger yard, about the size of two tennis courts. You'd get young lads walking fast, laughing and joking, then older ones who, if they were on the outside, the young lads would be going round them all the time, and they might have a crafty dig or something. So the old fellers walked further in, their heads down, trying to be invisible almost. I stayed on the outside usually, but often, if someone looked like they wanted to talk, I changed and went diagonal, or zig-zagged to be on me own

Colin

I was down the block four weeks, then given the choice to do the rest of my sentence, five years, down there, or transfer to VP's. There's an enormous stigma for a Mains prisoner to go to VP's, it's seen as being full of child molesters and rapists and you're frightened to be tarnished with the same brush. But I had a girlfriend when I came to prison and she swayed me. The block is the segregation unit within prison. You're kept in an isolation cell and you lose things like association, education, work, library and gym. If you're Good Order and Discipline, which was the case with me, you don't have to have broken any rules and you're down the block indefinitely. In the secure remand unit they'd kept me there for months, so when I landed down the block in high security it was a throwback. It affects people psychologically more then they'd admit, long periods of isolation. In that secure remand unit, some guy was noisy and the officers burst into his pad and kicked the shit out of him, so any interaction there is, it's negative.

Nigel

VP's tend to fall into two types; those that can't handle Main location and are moved there for their own protection, and then the majority, which are sex offenders. Both types are extremely manipulative and try to gain some form of control over any situation. That being said, they usually behave a lot better than Mains where it's an extremely volatile and challenging environment. I did two years solely on the Mains and preferred that to working on VP though, because I felt I could talk to them like men, unlike the VP's who are generally just sinister and nasty.

Antonio

We don't associate with VP's, ever. I've got a good anecdote though. In this high security prison the VP's were the kitchen workers, they cooked all the meals. One sunny day, the lads were out sunbathing and the screws walked past the fence with some unfortunate nonce.

All their heads turned and they nonced him off terrible. When he got to the end of the fence he stopped, then with a smirk on his face and loud as fuck he went, enjoy your tea lads. And that's all he had to say, they never ate off that servery for the three years I was in that jail. In the last prison I was in, it's the other way round, and a lot of lads working in the kitchens, I know them personally, and every chance they get to spit, piss or gob in food they know is going to the VP wing, they will take, without a shadow of a doubt. They're just normal boys off the council estates. Who wouldn't? Just read the fucking newspapers, there's some horrible bastards out there.

Billy

You don't know who you're talking to. There's probably loads of nonces walking among the general population, trying to get along with things. This lad told everyone he was in for Section 18, blah blah blah, you just believe people. Then one of the lads walked in with a newspaper and showed everyone. He'd got three years because he was on some order and the police knocked on his door and he had a fourteen year old boy locked in his cupboard. The lads walked up to his pad, because he was banged up, and said to his padmate, bash him or we'll do you. So his padmate brayed him all over.

Paige

I was on the quiet wing. The other wings were rowdy and there was always fights on them. I was on the quiet wing because I'd self-harmed when I first went in. But it was full of ex-druggies who would come in your pad begging for stuff. Someone tried to steal my jacket.

Val

Women who'd committed offences against their kids were red flagged. You never usually knew what they were in for, but you always got that creepy feeling. We raided their cells. This woman, she was always flanked by two officers and she was proper naughty. She'd been messing about with her daughter in front of a bloke, she done all sorts, shot everything at her. We tortured her. She killed herself in the end.

Billy

Sex offenders get brayed all the time. I've seen it happen loads, I've done it myself. This lad was on A wing. He'd raped someone and got six year, then got caught trying to rape a lass. I used to shake his hand on exercise, I thought he was a good kid. He said he'd stabbed a lad who'd nonced his sister. We were on exercise, and he'd been in a year, and he told me the lad he'd stabbed had just had his life support turned off. Nobody's on life support for a year, plus he wouldn't have been done for Section 18, he'd have been done for Attempted Murder. So when I had a visit with my brother, I said google his name and see what you find, I'll ring tomorrow and ask you a question. If you say yes, I know he's a nonce. If you say no, he's not. My brother answered the question with, yes definitely mate, one thousand percent, so I knew he was a bad nonce. I was about to get shipped out. I rang the bell and said, can I get a shower, I'm getting shipped out, I'll be in a paddy wagon all day. I said to that lad, come for a bit of crack in the shower mate, I'm getting shipped out tomorrow. So he came in the shower and I knocked him clean out, started punching him all over. Nobody even knew it was me.

Nigel

Very inappropriate types of conversation have to be stopped and challenged in VP classes, and these people are often inadequate and dirty. Mains are men, they take pride in themselves and make it very clear they're totally different to VPs. Mains tend to be gangsters, criminal organisation types and terrorists. But VP classes are a lot easier to handle, and so most teachers prefer to be on VP education for that reason.

Paige

I went to the library once but there was this famous child killer in there, so I never went back. She got slashed, in her face, so she stopped going to canteen but she went to the library. You used to see this other child killer as well, this paedophile, another famous one. She has privileges, she has five guards with her all the time, in the corridors, down the canteen, just because of people attacking her. She used to go past pregnant women and lick her lips and that, it was horrible.

Colin

I ran campaigns against paedophiles in the community, I saw them as worse than animals, so it was a major step for me to go to VP's. The people I interacted with first were all ex-Mains prisoners, they'd got into drug debts and run off because of punishment beatings and the risk of being stabbed. I wasn't allowed to work when I first landed, I guess they didn't trust me, because some prisoners do come down from Mains and bully or attack VP's. It took a few months and I was never trusted for some jobs. I was a wing cleaner on the Mains but I wasn't allowed that job on VP, because you're out your cell most the day, you're more of a security risk. Cleaners are the couriers in prisons, they have free run of the wings, they pass messages, smokes and drugs from door to door. Then I became interested in what made people tick, I talked to people on a personal level, whatever their crime. I played chess with a notorious child killer and at one point I'd have been ready to kill him. He came across as very intelligent and he won the chess game. We had discussions about the death penalty and he agreed with it and thought he should have got it, which surprised me enormously. I agree with him, but you can't have a death penalty with the corrupt system we have now, with the media deciding the outcome of trials and exaggerations and downright lies by police.

They Bang You Up

John

I was good at two things; music and looking after people. I applied for student nursing but was told boys didn't become nurses, so I joined the army as a musician and doubled up as a medic. Ten years later, in 1993, I'd trained as a nurse and was working in a hospital when a mate said, do you want a job in the prison service? I went in and I was horrified, it was like walking through stables. In the hospital wings the little observation flaps are big observation flaps you can pull right down, and all the prisoners had their heads out looking at me. Seriously, you could have put a nose bag on them. But they said, can you start Monday? We're short of nurses. And that was it, no interview, I'd got the job.

Sarah

They had an open day at the local leisure centre in 1994 because the new prison was opening. Thousands turned up. I started in payroll. Six months later, the prisoners arrived and it was quite exciting. The offices overlook the reception area, so we were all at the windows as the vans were coming every ten minutes. There was a huge turnover of staff the first twelve months, I did the wages so I knew. You're not taken as seriously because it's private, not HMP. You're not properly trained and it was common knowledge you were on rubbish money and everything was on the cheap. A lot of staff did the training, then went to HMP as soon as they could.

John

I became confident pretty much straight away because I realised these lads were vulnerable and as scared as I was, they were in the hospital wing for good reason. Eighteen months down the line, my Principal Officer said, if you do officer training we'll combine both, you'll become a hospital officer. I thought yeah, I'll be in a prison uniform so I'll have that respect, but I'll still be nursing. It took me ten years to realise it's impossible to be both, you can't sit with somebody who's cut their arms and then at half four say, right, behind your door, I'll see you in fifteen hours. So I applied to go on the wings and I've done a further eleven years as a fully-fledged officer, doing drug courses, induction courses, anything that doesn't involve opening and closing a door. I wanted to do something that taxed me, because I'm a reasonably intelligent bloke and I didn't want to be a turn-key.

Sarah

Every so often, they had courses to recruit prison officers and after three years on payroll, I fancied something different. The eight weeks training was quite intense. There were courses every six months because some people realised pretty quickly they weren't cut out for it, they gave it two months and were gone. But eventually they got people who were committed to the job, the discipline was there and they had regular staff on regular wings who built rapport with prisoners. You can never show anyone you're frightened, that's your biggest mistake. If they know they have you, that's it. You have to stand your ground, be firm but fair. Women are better at de-escalating situations. If officers are sat at a table, prisoners always make a beeline for the female. They see females as motherly figures, whereas the men, it's all aggression and in your face.

Colin

I've met officers you can talk to, but they're not anybody you could trust. Some try and paint the picture they are, that they're just one of the lads. Some are sadists, downright arseholes who take some sort of sick pleasure out of making people's lives a misery. In the secure remand unit, I'd managed to get on the wing, after much pressure from my solicitors who'd stated I was down the block for no reason. But they still kept me on twenty-four hour bang-up, they just brought my meals to the cell, threw it on the floor and slammed the door. I wasn't allowed exercise, I wasn't allowed showers, I wasn't allowed to clean my cell. And when you're Cat A, you're subject to strip searches and cell searches as often as they like, and they do it at least once a month. They moved me to another cell while they searched mine, and when I went back, they'd stolen the sheets off my bed. I asked where they'd gone and they said there were no sheets in the whole prison, I had to sleep directly on the mattress. This Supervising Officer said it was wrong, the way I was being treat, and he was trying to get it stopped, but it stayed the same, nothing changed until I was transferred out.

Billy

A lot of the younger screws were alright. The older ones had had enough and weren't passionate about their job. They just come to work because it's a job. The older screws were set in their ways and spoke to you like shit. They forgot you were a human being. Basically, there were more bad screws than good.

Donna

Some prison officers go out of their way, with a woman, to be some macho shit and show you up. Stick a uniform on and they grow a second dick. And then you get some women officers; what is that all about? Instead of just being a woman going about their job, it's like they have twice as much to prove. Then you have others who actually care about people. Generally, those in the sentence planning process are interested and have a different mentality, but you go on the wings and it's lock them up and chuck the key away. And if you think about it, they're getting less pay, less pension, conditions are worse, so people who are slightly more enlightened simply won't go for that role. It's not good. You could be stacking shelves in Tesco's one week, then working in a high security prison, with the country's most dangerous people, the next.

Alice

The whole system, the whole attitude, is geared to get the bastards in, lock them up and make our job as easy as possible. Education? Yeah, we'll give you classes, but there's a resentment attitude with some of the officers because some of the men become more educated than them, so a lot of them have this inferiority complex or feel threatened, and that brings out a passive-aggressive attitude. I remember one of the men doing A' Level Business Studies, a young black man who was part of the gang culture, quite aggressive at times, even in the classroom. I'd worked on strategies, how to handle him and develop a good rapport, and he got an A grade. I went on the wing and asked an officer to take me to his cell so I could give him the good news. The officer's reaction was obscene, I couldn't believe it. He opened the cell door and I told the man who was overjoyed. But the officer's face went red with anger, and he said something like, it's a waste of time, why should he get all this attention and education? All of the officers weren't like that, but a good number were. The good officers were mostly the older ones, who knew the value of rehabilitation. Maybe life had mellowed them out as they'd got older.

Stephen

What do we expect of prison officers? If we expect the things I think we should be expecting, then we don't give them enough training. But the Prison Officers Association's position seems to be that they simply lock people up and that is their core job. A recent POA statement said suicide prevention is an optional extra. Personally I think that's pretty shameful. If that's an optional extra, like hostage negotiation, then maybe we do give prison officers enough training after all.

Craig

The wing screws, one or two might talk pleasant, but they're constantly watching you for everything you say, everything you do, so you don't communicate because it might be used or wrote down. And you're observed constantly, every corridor there's cameras. When you're behind your door, they're checking the flap three or four times during the night, and every fifteen minutes in the hospital ward. The light's always on. You're just getting to sleep and the flap goes, then they make a point of slamming it shut so you wake up.

Antonio

Twenty percent of officers, maybe fifteen, are ex-military lads just doing a job, you know, crack on mate. They see us smoking a joint and they're not arsed, just look, don't drop me out, don't make a cunt of me in front of the cameras. A don't fuck with me, we won't fuck with you relationship, and they're cool. The rest are mostly dicks.

Peter

In the past, prison officers tended to have done national service, spent time in uniform and like the camaraderie, the element of physical danger and muscular rehabilitation, and love, even pathologically need, the opportunity to be better than others. They'd refer to prisoners as scum and pond life. If, for no other reason than the eradication of national service, that's changed a bit. Prison Officers have a wider view than they did, although any residential work is introspective and to some extent xenophobic. It's not a job I would fancy, it's a thankless task and one in which you're increasingly exposed to risk.

Colin

It's more tense on Mains, there's more gangs and an overtone of threat. It exists on VP's but it's not as prevalent. Prison officers act differently as well. On VP's they're harder and have a more negative attitude, they bully and wind the prisoners up more. I've heard prison officers call inmates 'fucking nonces' countless times, whereas on the

Mains they're more guarded because the prisoners are physically more dangerous. I've been there when prison officers have been stabbed, I've seen it happen, and they run the risk of having to deal with gangs rather than individuals, as would be more likely on VP's. This prison officer was overly zealous and too forthright, in people's faces and their business. People were shitting and pissing in a bucket and keeping it stashed, and someone who had an issue with drugs was paid to throw it over her.

Billy

They're that understaffed, they haven't got the time of day for you. In one prison, there was two hundred prisoners on a wing, easy, and you'd only have three or four staff walking about when we were all out our cells on association. They're running to other wings because someone's fighting. You'd have a prisoner asking them to put credit on their phone, a prisoner asking for new kit, and they haven't the time to do it.

Sarah

Training and putting things into practice are totally different. In real life, you've got seconds to think about what you're doing, it's frightening. You try and talk them down and ninety percent of the time it works, but not the other ten percent. After a period of time you get used to it, it's an adrenalin rush, because usually it's mundane, walking around the wing, locking and unlocking. I'm not saying you look forward to things happening but when something goes off, that's when you become a good team, when your colleagues have got your back.

Craig

You get your dinner, they bang you up. You get your tea, they bang you up. They open doors and let you out for an hour, so you can have a shower or go on the exercise yard. Sometimes, depending on the weather, exercise might only be quarter of an hour. Sometimes you walk past the screws, go down to the gates, which by rights should be open for you, but if there's nobody waiting to go out, the screws haven't left where they're sat. You think, am I pissing them off wanting to be out? When it was only me I sometimes wouldn't bother, but that backfired because next time they wouldn't get up, and they can see you stood at the gate waiting, but they look and keep talking, or get up as if they're going to let you out and then make a cup of tea instead. And there's loads of that, chipping away all the time to get you more and more angry. But you can't let it get to you, you've got to rise above it.

Stephen

I'd get onto the wing and say I'm here to see Mister Jones, and the officers would say, the only misters here are us, he's Jones 2345. One, it was showing contempt for the people they work for, and two, it was an attempt at bullying me. They were basically saying, unless you ask properly, we're not going to get him. They use these ludicrous terms. I'm a 'civilian.' I told them, we're both civilians. They said, we wear a uniform. They do that in Sainsbury's, I said, what's the difference? They struggled to answer. It's a pseudo-military thing, and the language reflects that. What concerns me is that it's a driver to otherness and I don't think it serves anyone well.

Alice

I was looking for a prisoner to give Open University material to, and I have a habit of calling prisoners Mister Whatever, because I'm aware they never get their full title. Some might say, why would you give respect to a criminal? But I'm not dealing with criminals, I'm dealing with human beings who have committed crimes, who are in prison being punished by being deprived of their freedom, but are also being rehabilitated, and education's part of that. So I went into the gym to give this guy his stuff. I went to the officers and said, this is for Mister Whatever. And they were astounded. Mister? There's no Misters in here. I said, well I choose to call them Mister. And so he yelled out his surname, and I thought, I'm going to keep doing my bit here, and keep being respectful. The thing is, officers who are ignorant mix that up with condoning crime. I would never condone any criminal activity, I abhor all types of violence. And that's the problem; they can't separate the human being from the person who committed the crime. But you've got to treat that person with humanity, within the prison system.

Paige

Some of the teachers were alright, it was the guards that were arseholes. There was two females and one male on our wing. There was never more than one male, ever. And the males were arseholes, they treat you like scum. The females were a bit more understanding. But none of them help at all, not really.

What would have been helpful?

If they'd listened to me, because they knew everything I'd went through. But they didn't.

Donna

Most officers don't have communication skills. And what they do, and oh this is horrible, they work them. You've not had a letter from the wife? Well, we know what she'll be doing then. And when they react, they're banged up or get another year on their sentence. It's a different world, honest. You've got the academia world of prison, what they teach in criminology etc, and then there's the real world, people who work in prisons and know prisons. They're completely different. I was seeing this category A prisoner, a huge feller who'd murdered twice inside and raped, but he'd turned to Buddhism. They had glass interview rooms with electronic doors, so we're sitting there, and if you didn't move the lights went off. The officer's outside supposed to be watching us, but the lights kept going off, and the lad kept jumping up to get them back on. I'm saying to him, can you pack that in? Every time you do that, understandably with your background, you're frightening the shite out of me. Then I'm knocking on the glass door to get this officer's attention because I couldn't open it from the inside, and he didn't even respond, he was reading the newspaper. This feller said, I could do anything to you. In the end, the officer finally opened the door. I contacted the governor and he said, well you know, mistakes happen.

Peter

Michael Howard did away with the CQSW, the old social work route into probation, and I'm not in principle against having specific qualifications, but at the same time the Prison Officers Association was successfully resisting the introduction of a minimum education requirement of two GCSE's to become a prison officer, stating life experience was more important. But there should be a degree or equivalent course, two or three years of vocational and academic training, for people to become prison officers. It's a very complex task, and the more understanding they have of what they do and the implications of the way they do it, the far better we'd be protected. And that's Holland, that's Sweden, that's Belgium, that's a range of other countries.

Keith

We've changed the selection criteria for officers now, it's gone up to five GCSE's. But when I was Governor 4 at this high security prison we had one officer who was a five-foot ex-miner who could twist prisoners around his finger just by the way he spoke to them. And yet the likes of him wouldn't get in now, because he never had qualifications, just a great personality, interpersonal skills and a sense of humour. Now we've got people coming in with degrees. Are they really going to be satisfied in a few years when the promotion prospects aren't there? We've been vastly reducing the size of our workforce, so there's far less opportunities for promotion. You can understand why people don't see it as a career anymore.

John

Eighty percent of prison officers are good people. Ten percent come in as good people, get pips on their shoulders and become bad. The other ten percent are simply spoiling for a fight. They know they can legitimately get hold of somebody, punch somebody, and they can cover it on a piece of paper and get away with it. These officers are in the minority but we know who they are. If there's an incident and you're on with someone, you'll know how they're going to react. I get called names because I'd rather stand sideways and have a chat with someone than jump on them. If a prisoner is getting hold of me, or having a go, another prisoner will likely come up and say, he's alright, leave him alone. But others, they'll just close the door and let them crack on. But why go into work and punch somebody when there's ninety-four others on the wing that know you've done it? It's ridiculous. Some staff won't even talk to me. I was friends with one on Facebook, then there was an incident and I refused to involve myself because it was wrong. He deleted me as a friend and wouldn't talk to me again, even at work. But if something kicks off on the wing I can't distance myself from it. If a prisoner's banged up or taken back from his visit early, he won't have a go at me less because of who I am, but he won't punch me, whereas he might somebody else. I still get the verbal, but maybe next morning he'll say, sorry boss, I was out of order. And at the end of the day, I want to walk through Tesco and not have somebody hit me over the head with a bottle because of what I've done three years ago. There are times you have to get your hands on, of course there are, but I'm not a fan.

Keith

I'm sure violence from officers was common twenty years ago, but I'd be very surprised if that was still the case. We've got so much CCTV coverage it would be extremely difficult to get away with it. Besides, we've changed the whole recruitment process, we look at the psychology of individuals these days. When I joined, the vast majority of officers were ex-forces, they had a completely different mentality. Now, we've got graduates who want to help people, not beat them up. Times have changed. We may still have a few bad apples in the system, but nowhere near as many.

Stephen

If you look at the narrative on prisons and safety, at the moment a very powerful narrative, the statistics and discussions omitted from that are prison officer assaults on prisoners. It's not discussed because it's somehow disloyal to staff. Narratives are powerful because they're value laden and are therefore fiercely protected, for all sorts of good reasons, but we should unpack them and have real discussions. I've been involved in numerous investigations and it's striking how people suddenly develop significant disabilities in terms of vision and hearing. It's not exclusive to prisons, it's an organisational dynamic. But just as prisoners say they don't like grasses, so it is with prison staff. We need to structure things accordingly because it's very hard to find out things when officers behave badly.

Craig

It reminded us of being at the farm. You'd have a hundred cows. Each cow would have its own identity, but it was just get in, get milked and get on with it. You end up being programmed the same. I opened gates for cows and they knew to go to a certain stall and stand there for milking, you didn't need to tell them. So once I got into the habit of it, I knew it was my job to walk there, or there. It didn't matter whether I wanted to or not, when that door opened I did whatever was required. They herded us to certain places and herded us back again.

Val

There was only one screw who was really nasty. She worked in the gym in the open prison and there was something wrong with her head. She said, you need to get that fucking chip off your shoulder. I said, well you won't be the one to fucking do it. She hated me, she told me as well. And she always got me for piss tests, and I never took drugs in there, or drunk. She waited until she knew I'd been to the toilet, got me, then stood over me and watched. I used to say to her, I bet you get great joy in this, don't you? And you have to strip when they do cell searches, that's the worst part about jail, because you've got no dignity. You're stood there with nothing on while they're stripping your bed.

Paige

This girl told the governor when a female guard done something to her. So the guard got two prisoners to jump on her and bash her in. But it was all the male guards who were proper arsey, and some of the women ones were actually alright.

Stephen

When I asked prison officers about how many staff they thought were suitable for particular wings, the response was never a number, it was who they were working with. When they came on duty, they looked at the list, and with some individuals thought, actually I'd rather not have them here. They were far more focused on the quality of their colleagues than the numbers of them, even though there has to be a sense of how many officers you need to run a wing.

Sarah

Some officers are definitely up for giving prisoners a good hiding, but not as much as before because there's different people now and they haven't the control and back-up. Before, you knew if your back was covered by who you were on with, and regardless of who the officer and prisoner was, I was up for it, because that's just me as a person. Now they'd sooner walk away from it because of new staff and how few of us there are. If prisoners refuse education they should be banged up, but certain staff would be on the two days you were off, and they couldn't be arsed because it's easier to just leave them on the landing. I'd come back and try banging them up, and they'd say, I've been out for the last two days, that officer's not bothered. I'd say, it's either education, work or bang-up, you know how it goes. I went to put one prisoner behind his door, he tried to smash me in the face with a flask of hot water and it kicked off. There was loads of people out on the landing and believe it or not, the two male officers I was on with, one ran off the wing and the other hid under the staircase. I was grappling on the floor with this guy. I called for response but it was two prisoners that helped me, not my own colleagues, people I'd got a bit of rapport with that thought, Jesus, there's a woman down there and she's getting assaulted. Two staff ran up from downstairs and one of them got a broken jaw. I've been on the sick since, because it wasn't the first time these two officers had left me in a dangerous situation, and I can't work with people I know aren't covering my back. I asked one why he'd ran off. He said, my head's gone, and he had a nervous breakdown after that. The other said he feared for his own safety. If it wasn't for prisoners coming to help me, God knows what would have happened.

Daniel

Prisoners are not all scum you know, like they're made out to be. If I'd been on the wing, with some officer I liked, and he was attacked, I'd have stopped it. If they're alright with me, and I'm alright with them, I don't want anything to happen to them. Prisoners look after people if they're alright with them, just like they look after their mates.

In Your Pocket

Peter

Crime in general is about drugs, isn't it? Drugs and a lack of constructive activities. At one point in my career I gave myself a little mission to work with drug related house burglary, because if I make the wrong choice over a shop-lifter and a high street store gets harmed, I'm not celebrating that but I'll sleep easy. But if I take a chance on somebody and people's homes get screwed, I've been burgled myself, three times, I know what it's like. Every Christmas, as I put my key in the lock, I go to check the presents I've hid behind the wardrobe are still there. It ripples. And it's more than twenty years since the last time I was burgled. But effective drug treatment is an awful lot more than just prescribing substitute medication and testing. We might be happy to call it that, but it's not, it's social control at best, and it's not very good at that. And don't you love those drug workers? Cuddly drugs workers that say, I've got such a good relationship with them, and you think yeah, they'd have a good relationship with me if I was giving them free drugs.

Daniel

The drugs scene in high security is more prescription drugs than anything else, it's just junkies. When people are on medication, they hide it under their tongue and save them up for a week. Muslim gangs don't have anything to do with that, it's more whites, or black lads that haven't converted, because there are loads that haven't. Drugs do come in from outside, but when you're in high security, visits are hard work. If class A drugs come onto the wing, it hasn't come from visits, it's been brought in by somebody who works there. You can never pinpoint who exactly has brought it in, but it's definitely not prisoners or their families. I know somebody who went on a visit in high security, and they smuggled one ecstasy tablet in for New Year's Eve , one, and he was thought of as a God. Honestly, it was unbelievable, everyone was thinking he was fucking Houdini or something.

John

Prisons are rife with drugs. Years ago, I walked around the wing at night, smelled cannabis and thought so be it, if it keeps them quiet. When I first started they didn't have televisions in their cells, and when they said everyone was getting one we were up in arms. Then they all got televisions and I was on nights and it was silent, it was fantastic. And I thought God, what were we complaining about? Cannabis had the same effect. So low level drugs, I don't give a hoot about, but there's people dying now with what used to be called legal highs, and when it starts getting dangerous and people are getting taxed and slashed for it, then it's got to be controlled. Mandatory drug testing meant prisoners changed to heavier drugs, and that brought more violence and other problems. Cannabis stays in your system for twenty-eight days and heroin is something like seventy-two hours. The punishment for both is the same, so why would you risk things for cannabis? And then legal highs came in and they couldn't test for them. And in all honesty, if I was in prison, I would look for an easy option to deal with things.

How do drugs get into prisons?

Officers. Visits. Being chucked over or posted in. More officers bring stuff in than civvie staff, it's easier for them. One officer brought a kebab in every week, and obviously we had dogs on the gate, but the dogs sniffed the kebab and everyone thought nothing of it. The drugs were inside the kebab. LSD came under stamps, we had to take the stamps off all the letters. Children's paintings came in and in the paint was cocaine mixed with water. The best one I ever saw was a pigeon. Someone was feeding a pigeon with bits of chicken or whatever, then they threaded a blanket so they had thirty metres of thread. They tied it to whatever they were feeding the pigeon with, the pigeon picked it up, they clapped and the pigeon flew over the wall so they had a line over the wall. Someone came out of B&Q and tied it to whatever they wanted. So yeah, training a pigeon. When you're using babies and nappies and things, it's a different ball game, but when you're training a pigeon, that's brilliant.

Daniel

How can prisons deal with drugs? Prison officers nowadays aren't the same as when I first went to prison. Then, if they thought you had drugs in your cell, when everyone got locked up, you'd have ten officers in your cell, ripping it to bits. Nowadays, look in any newspaper or go online and look at what you need to become a prison officer in a private prison. They're employing people that are nineteen, twenty year old. One of the lads employed before I left, he was nineteen year old and nine stone, he'd just finished working in Carphone fucking Warehouse. When you was a prison officer back in the day, you wanted to be a prison officer because it was a career, whereas nowadays these young lads are just using it as a stopgap until they get something else, and they're only getting nineteen grand a year. As soon as you know that, you can turn them. Look, you say, if you're only here for a few years, I'll give you a grand if you bring me a forty pound phone in. I know it sounds a lot of money, but as soon as he brings that phone in and you've paid him a grand, that's it, he's in your pocket. You can say, I want this bringing in, I want that bringing in, because otherwise I'm telling them about the phone, and I haven't even touched it since you give it me, so it's got your fingerprints all over it. I had a prison officer bring me strawberries and cream when Wimbledon was on. I liked Listerine mouthwash, but you can't get it because it's got alcohol in, she brought that in. I never got her to bring me drugs in, or a mobile phone because I had that anyway, but everything else, the home comforts I missed, I had fucking braised steak and mashed potato once.

Billy

There were phones on the wing and I'm not being funny, it's a Cat B HMP prison, it's not easy to smuggle phones into there, even up your arse, it doesn't happen. You have to sit down on the boss chair when you come in, and it detects any metal inside you. It was officers that did it. People can chuck stuff over the walls but this prison was in the city centre and the police station's a hundred yards away.

Antonio

There was this black kid, some alley boy, a new kid in class. He was in my chair and I'd sat there for years, so I asked him to move but he wouldn't, and a couple of the black lads were waiting to see what my reaction was. I said, fucking get up now or I'll throw you out. He was a dangerous kid, with a knife and whatever, but he'd just come from the streets of London and I looked at his arms and neck and belly and they were soft. I was looking to see where I could damage him and I knew I had the strength to do it, maybe not now because he's got a thirty year rec, he'll be fucking strong now, but he'd only just started his sentence. He moved straight away and apologised, and the reason I'm telling you this is that he was one of the main drug suppliers. For one ounce of Spice, five, six thousand in there, two hundred out here. So he's a popular black boy him, and he'd only just arrived in that prison and everybody was up his arse. I seen him a few times in the gym after and eventually he started making sure I had a spliff now and then.

Colin

There was lots of heroin on the Main wing. People took it to get through their sentence, they established their drug addiction in a high security prison. And if people don't pay their debts then it's easy to get someone stabbed, you just offer a tenner bag and addicts will do anything, including assault officers. That's a prison tenner bag of course, there's a lot less drugs in it than there would be on the outside, and a lot more brick dust. A female officer was bringing heroin in. She stood guard at cells while phone calls were made on contraband mobiles, while drugs were passed on. She stood guard while people were beaten for drug debts, she was getting paid for that too. She got suspended and moved to another prison to hush it up. It was obvious to everyone what was happening. There's dealers in high security prisons who've made millions. Some of them are big and intimidating and there's no place to hide when officers are helping dealers with punishment beatings. There's a lot of looking the other way, trying to find a happy medium to keep the peace. And if someone's beating the shit out of another inmate, well at least it's not happening to an officer. Because who cares about an inmate? Nobody, inside or out.

Daniel

So drugs aren't rife in high security, but they are in other jails, and it's mainly Spice nowadays. Out here you can buy a gram for twenty quid. In jail, you'd get two hundred for it. Subutex, you get out here for next to nothing, but in Jail one Subby is a tenner. Some people get out of jail, get loaded up with Subbies and Spice and get recalled on purpose. And if I had a problem, I'd find some Spice or Smack addict, wait until they had none and say, look, I've got some here, but I want you to smack something around his head. And they'd do it, so somebody else was doing my dirty work while I'm looking like an angel.

Billy

There was fights every other day in adult prison, it was nuts. It was about drugs mainly. People used to get out on licence, pack drugs up their arse and get recalled to sell them. Or if people knew they were getting sent down from court, they'd do that first. Prison was a hotbed for drugs. I was padded up with a couple of druggies and they were either monged out or up a height, it was odd. This lad next door made loads of hooch (*homemade alcohol using fruit juice*) and he sold it because he had a Subutex habit. There was always fights and slashings over drugs.

Paige

It's easy to smuggle drugs, lasses just pouch them. When newbies come in they just stash them up their bits, because they can't search them there. And there was a lot of drugs inside, a lot.

Keith

Drugs have always been a major issue. The environment has changed and the atmosphere is very volatile. Mandatory drug testing isn't really effective and is a resource issue itself, because we can only afford to test five to ten percent of the population. And it's always been the case that the dealers in prison don't use drugs. We pick up users at the bottom end of the feeding chain, but the dealers get away with it, and it's them we really need to focus on. We've got drones bringing drugs over prison walls, dead pigeons full of drugs being thrown over the wall so cleaners can pick them up. Preventing drugs from getting into prisons is nigh on impossible, so education has to be the way forward. When we created a therapeutic community in the female prison we saw a massive decrease in drugs, because people began to realise the damage they'd done to themselves and to friends and families.

Adele

Drugs and alcohol are the reasons the vast majority of these lads are inside. The Spice that's going on now, it's the worst I've ever seen, it's horrendous. A guy who's been in and out of there for years, he's six foot four and hammers the gym, he's never disrespectful but he'll take anything. His mum was terminally ill and he stole her morphine. When she died, the will was divided between him and his sister, who was straight as a die. If he stayed out of prison he got one thousand pounds a month. If he was in prison he got one hundred. He'd be out, spend that thousand on drugs, then come back in to a hundred. He was running around the wing, totally naked, he smashed the television and assaulted four staff, then went down the block and two days later had no recollection of it at all. The Spice killed him, he's dead now. And the men are talking about it like, why wouldn't you take it? I was asleep and I woke up and I thought I was covered in spiders and that my pad-mate was trying to kill me. But why? Why would you want to feel like that? I don't understand. Yeah, but it gets a couple of nights over, doesn't it?

The government has changed the law regarding 'legal highs,' or Novel Psychoactive Substances as we're supposed to call them. Now, on the outside, it's illegal to supply but not to have personal possession, but inside prisons it's illegal for personal possession as well as supplying. Has that made any difference?

NPS, that's what we call them. We've got posters saying what it can do to them. We've had staff briefings on how to recognise if someone's under the influence. There's been staff affected by it, when they've inhaled it, but it's very hard to detect on a drugs test.

Have there been any arrests inside the prison?

Arrests? Inside a prison?

Well it's a criminal offence now, to be in possession of NPS inside prison.

There's so few staff, they wouldn't have the time. Drugs are out of control. Sometimes, when all the prisoners are out on association, there's only four to six staff. What can they do?

Daniel

I've seen people in local prisons off their rockers on Spice, and I mean off their fucking rockers. I'd never even heard of it before I went there. I saved somebody's life when they overdosed on it. He was on the floor having a fit, he'd stopped breathing and went blue, and none of the prisoners would fetch a fucking screw because they were scared of getting their cell busted. So I put a spoon in his gob, stopped him from swallowing his tongue, put him in the recovery position, found a screw and said, you need to get someone up here quick, he's fucked. And do you know what I got for saving his life? A bottle of pop. They were fucking lucky it were a woman who give it me, I was expecting a C Cat.

John

On nights, you patrol the outside of the grounds. You watch drugs and stuff flying over the wall in packets, inside tennis balls. It's fascinating standing there, watching it all, everyone shouting out their cells, their ingenuity is phenomenal. I step out the shadows and grab the ball and they shout, ah you cunt Mr H. Things coming between cells as well, on the outside walls, every cell with a bit of string from one to another. And watching on the landings when a mirror comes out tied to a bit of string, slid from one side of the landing to the other under the door, little things coming with it. You spoil their fun by standing on it and get a torrent of abuse for half an hour. But then they laugh and say, I nearly got away with it Mr H, you're on the fucking ball again.

Peter

Most of the guys I'm writing for are going to jail and will be supervised on licence by the National Probation Service. A shoplifter doing drug related inquisitive crime; he definitely needs testing and maybe needs group-work and constructive activities, so there's three agencies involved there. What he'll tend to get is prescribing and testing, because that's an absolute minimum and you can only go so far without the carrot of free drugs. People keep appointments for free drugs, and you'll be providing a review for the court, so given there's no sanction for on-going drug use they haven't much to lose by being tested. A group-work programme's expensive, and plugging them into another agency for constructive activity's expensive, so maybe they won't happen, or we'll turn to the cheaper of the two. But unless you've got something to put in the hole of the doughnut, they're only going to fill it with illicit drugs aren't they? Many of the people I work with have this huge sense of entitlement, drug users particularly, because with drugs you get the illusion of something for nothing, in order to feel better all I have to do is take this thing. Nobody gets a long term drug dependency because they're having a good relationship with themselves. People come to you and go, if I can just get that help I need. Where is that help? Tell me about it? And they can rarely join it up, because what they're actually saying is, if somebody can just do this for me, and I can wake up in a month's time clean, then I think it would all be solved. But actually it wouldn't be, you'd just be a month clean. The monkey might be off your back but the circus is still in town, and it's doing cartwheels between your ears because you need a whole new set of life skills, because the ones you've got won't necessarily translate.

Damage

Sarah

We were a Cat A prison when we first opened, but we lost it after five years and became Cat B. The Home Office said we weren't fit to house Cat A anymore. I worked with juveniles, we had them when we first opened as well, but they stopped them after a few years when they realised how bad they were. The violence was terrible. You know what youngsters are like, they argue if they've got one sausage less than somebody else, they're in your face all the time. If they didn't have a job back then, they'd be out all day on association, but they realised there was no incentive for education or work, and loads would just sit on the wing all day, so it changed and if you didn't go to education or work it was bang-up. You got a lot of trouble then, people refusing to bang-up, but if they don't have money sent in, they have nothing for phone calls or canteen, and they get paid for attending work or education. It was only fifty pence a day but it's gone up to two pounds now. You get your food of course, and it's pretty good for prison, you get five choices for your dinner. It's £1.67 per day, per person, which isn't much, but there's lots of people better off in there than they are outside, food-wise. When the juveniles went we had separate wings for sex offenders. Everybody was mingled together at the start and there was lots more trouble. Every house-block had four wings, two up, two down. One wing had juveniles and the wing above had sex offenders,. The juveniles just waited for sex offenders to come off the wing and gave them a good hiding. You still get sex offenders on normal location if they want to be there, they have to apply for VP wings. Some of them say they're in for drink driving or whatever and get away with it, but some get found out.

Billy

There was this lad working on the servery, he looked a bit mental. One of the lads told me he'd raped his little brother. I said, what, and you're allowing him to work here? I'm not working with a fucking nonce. So they said to this lad, who owed money to them, snap a pool cue over his head on association and we'll write the debt off. The lad ran over and snapped the fucking cue right over the back of his head and started punching him all over. All the screws rushed in. The next day, they said to this other lad, we'll write your debts off if you boot him in the face and punch him all over. So he did, even though the screws were sat next to him. The lads who did it got took straight down the block and got another twenty-eight days inside instead of being out on licence.

Antonio

Lots of people thought it useful to be my friend, but I would only be theirs if it was useful for me, so it was reciprocal, it was as clinical as that on both sides.

In what ways could someone be useful to you?

If they work in the kitchens they can bring me food, spices, meat. If they work in education they can bring paper, books, pens. If they're a good cook they can make me dinner. If their food-bolt does a fried breakfast on a Sunday morning they can bend me in on it and I can get a breakfast on Sunday for fuck all. If someone gets weed, he can give me a spliff every time he sees me. There could be a million reasons. But if he's getting the shit kicked out of him by the screws, I'll walk past cold as fuck because he aint that kind of mate. There are several mates though, that if anyone touches a hand on them, it's on, and we're all watching out for each other.

What was different about them?

Some were from my area. One had my back, unexpectedly, even though he was terrified. Someone had nicked my phone, a contraband, and was renting it out. Wrighty brought it to me and said, I believe this is yours. I said, it fucking is, who's renting you that? He said, that

black kid there. I looked in the kitchen and it was full of big black mus-
cly lads, it couldn't have been a worse situation. I said, I'm going in
there to speak to him. He said, no, don't go in. I said, I'm going in
there right fucking now, because I had to do it on the spur of the moment, even though every fibre in my body was saying don't. So I got
something to defend myself with and I went and spoke to him, and
Wrighty came with me and he was shaking, and he'd only been on the
wing a couple of weeks. This black kid basically crumbled and apologised. He had a really good excuse and he was hugging me. Another
time Wrighty was on the wing and someone was slagging me off and
he sorted it. Someone bad mouthed me, someone close to me, in front
of everybody. Wrighty said, you wouldn't fucking say that if he was on
the landing. This guy was a dominant bloke and could have knocked
him out, and nobody else said it but Wrighty did. And it got back to me
and I thought, go on son.

Nigel

Violence in high security prisons is something that doesn't happen
as often as you might think. I've been there five years and there's been
very little. But gangs are a reality and the violence that does occur is
brutal to say the least. It's often gangs using debt to instigate assaults
and retribution on people.

Billy

One lad was shouting out his door, I'll see you on exercise next
morning, I'll fucking kill you. I'd bashed his mate in the shower. I said,
don't go on about it mate, just fucking do it in the morning. But the
screws came to my pad with food and wouldn't let me out. I said, you
can fucking keep it, because if I haven't seen it put on my plate I don't
know what you've done to it. Then in the morning they moved me to
another wing and wouldn't let me out on exercise, but there's this big
road round the prison where everyone walks to education, and I saw

that lad. I said, come on then, shouting out your window, do it. I was on basic anyway, and I was going to get another twenty-eight days for bashing his divvy mate up. He said, sorry mate, I didn't realise it was you. You get loads like that, acting as if they're game for anything when they're behind their doors. That's what happened with his mate. I told him to pipe down because he was making a racket when everyone was trying to sleep. He said, I'll meet you in the shower in the morning. But he wouldn't. So when I saw him walk in, I walked after him and started punching him all over. It's just what happens.

Daniel

The gangs in high security are basically Muslim or non-Muslim, but most of them aren't Muslim, they just think they are. These black lads that convert, they only do it to feel part of a gang like outside, because you need protection in high security. It was basically us against them, like a battlefield. But if we had a problem with somebody, we'd go and fight them, whereas a Muslim isn't allowed to attack anybody without asking permission from the hierarchy first. And the high security estate is controlled, one hundred percent, by Muslims, believe me it's well known. They control it by where they eat, by fear, by what washing machines non-Muslims can use, it's crazy how much influence they have on the running of everyday life. They encourage people off VP by saying, turn Muslim and we'll protect you. They protect them for a while, give them food, clothes, make them feel part of the family, then it's right, you need to prove yourself, go stab him or throw hot oil over him. And they can't say no, they do it, get put back on VP's for their own protection and then they start on somebody else. It's mad how a gang like that is allowed to operate how it does, in a British prison. Most people turning Muslim now, they do it just to feel safe.

Nigel

The terrorists are usually polite and respectful, but they're still dangerous men who could cause mayhem if they wanted to. I think a prison within a prison could stop radicalising as they won't have access to the general population and the staff on that unit will be trained to deal with the issue. Behaviour has to be controlled and I think it's a good idea.

Alice

I don't know enough about the decision to create prisons within prisons for extremist Muslims, but I do know it will be fraught with problems. A prison within a prison means depriving them of so much, and creating a potential for it to be a living hell hole. I think prison authorities overreact to the danger of proselytising and all of that. It's almost like you have a certain colour of skin and you're a danger. I don't even think it will work. Some people get converted into extremist forms of Islam, we know that, but I don't think this is the answer. You've got to keep a better eye on liaisons within prison, in all departments. I've contacted Security myself a couple of times when I felt certain parts of the prison population were attempting to bring others in, and I always had a high Muslim population in my classes.

Keith

Any prison within a prison needs to be subject to effective oversight by an appropriate Governor grade. I can understand the rationale in protecting other prisoners from being radicalised but this should not occur in a sterile and restricted environment. I remember the ethos of the special unit at Hull, with its aim of managing difficult prisoners but at the same time assisting them in resolving the issues that had led them there in the first place, and aiming for an eventual return to the main part of the prison. These planned units should have the same aims, coupled with a regime designed to de-radicalise those prisoners contained in there.

Antonio

There are tensions. It's exactly the same in prisons as it is in the community. There's loads of Africans who are Arabs, and therefore by default they're brothers with the Asian Arabs, and that's a pretty big gang. You get black kids off the streets of London, Manchester, Liverpool, Glasgow, whatever, they've got aunties and uncles in these African countries, so they're affiliated with the Muslim brothers because if they get with them boys they've got a big fucking back up. So yeah, throw into that mix the heady spice of extremism and the dislike for extremism amongst the British population. I tried to get on with them all. I got fed by the Muslim brothers and I ate a fried breakfast with the lads, their direct enemies. But that's a difficult path and I don't think it's common. I was disliked by several people because of that and if I wasn't such a big bloke, and wasn't so well spoken about by bigger men, I wouldn't have got away with it. Some of those big men still fell out with me over it, but that's their loss, I'm out here now and some of them got thirty-five fucking years. Why would you fall out with someone like me? I might be a fucking nobody, I might be a tramp and have hardly nothing but I can send you a pound. So yeah, I became entangled a little bit, and I just had to try and remain friends with everybody. But they are very violent places, high security prisons, and it's only gonna be a matter of time before there are deaths on a regular basis. There's lads who are never going home, who've already killed once or twice. I've seen people stabbed in the chest for a half ounce of tobacco. I was stabbed in the throat, within an inch of my artery, because a black boy thought I was a racist, and he was a cockney fucking rapist, who'd got all muscled and had the brothers on his side. Unfortunately for him he stabbed the wrong man, I smashed his head in. And when he went to the brothers, they said, oh fucking hell, he's actually alright him, you've done a wrong thing. We both ended up down the block but he never came out again. So yeah, it can go off in a blink.

But how much of all that is down to violent men? And how much of it is down to violent men in Muslim, black and white gangs?

Look, there was always violence in prisons and there always will be. Throw in drink, drugs, mental issues and bad blood off the street. You've got gangs from two sides of a city who are in for murdering each other. But the lack of weaponry stops there being as many deaths as there would be, it's difficult to find something big enough or sharp enough to kill quickly. There's lots of monitoring, and you know you've got to do it quick because it's all CCTV. But someone will get killed, and it could be officers, educational staff, other civvie staff. I'll give you a perfect example. A lad turns up for education induction on his second day, he's in the class when three of the gang he's in for shooting at, and killing one of their brothers, walk past. Within an hour he's getting smashed to fuck in the toilets. The teachers seen it, the officers seen it. If anybody tried to get involved they're possibly gonna get damage as well. So it's not necessarily about extremism, much as this day and age it's a topical subject. I suppose its raked it up by about an extra twenty-five percent, which is big, but there's another seventy-five percent.

Ivory Towers

Keith

I was an accountant for an engineering firm that found itself in difficulties. I wanted to stay in the same field but couldn't find anything that paid the same money or had the same family approach. Then I saw an advert for the prison service, joined as an officer and realised I preferred working with people more than numbers. I worked in a local prison from 1980 to 1983, then transferred to a mixed prison. I passed the entry tests to go into the governor grades, went away somewhere in the country, was interviewed by a governor, a psychologist and a senior civil servant, and took part in role plays and tests. That started off a three year sandwich course, where fourteen of us went to HMP Wakefield.

John

There are some good governors, very good ones, but there's cranks as well, we've had votes of no confidence in some. They used to do governor's rounds, but seeing the governor on your wing now is a very rare occurrence. The link's gone. The top three rungs of the ladder have disappeared. And there should be links right through, from top to bottom, you're there as a team. Governors these days are in their ivory towers. If there's a riot, you don't see them until everything's settled down. They used to show their face, you know, I'm here with you boys, but that doesn't happen anymore. And governors change all the time, they only stay at each prison two or three years, then they move sideways or upwards. If they're rubbish, they never go down, they get moved into another role. And that can't bring any benefits, when you've got officers who've been in one prison twenty, thirty years. You build respect with staff, don't you? If the management's constantly changing, it can't help. We had one governor that played Ride of the Valkyries at every staff meeting to inspire us. That's the last thing thirty hot-headed prison officers need when they're going back on the wings.

Keith

My first governor's post was as trainee assistant governor in Strangeways, Manchester, a huge local prison that locked up 1800 prisoners, sometimes three to a cell. The routine was slopping out, feeding and exercise, there was little work and it ground people down. I stayed there six years, went to a Young Offenders Institute for twelve months, then got promoted to Governor Four, as it was then, at a high security prison in 1990. There was such a lack of trust between staff and prisoners, it was a terrible atmosphere, and we lost D Wing for a while in a riot. Governor Three and I did most of the face-to-face stuff on the wing, meeting prisoners, adjudications, applications. Then I became head of inmate activities, industries and education, and did that until 1995.

Daniel

You see the governor once every three months when they make a brief visit to the wing. They get bombarded with questions from every prisoner, and they always give the same response, mention it to the officers. Number One governors are like David Cameron. They promise everything and deliver fuck all.

Billy

I saw governors a few times, because I was always put in front of them for fighting and stuff. The only other time I saw a governor was when one of them came to the induction class for ten minutes. You don't stand a chance when you're put in front of them. It's basically, the officer said that, so that's what it is. And officers have lied, they lie all the time. They always say they're going to sort stuff out for you and they never do. They tell a governor you said this and that, when you haven't. It doesn't matter what you say, you're getting done for it.

Keith

I needed to get a prison of my own and do some real governing. I was successful at interview and spent six years turning a female prison around. Rehabilitation was a concept nobody understood, but I got support from Probation and education. We got rid of male officers who didn't want to work with women, recruited thirty-odd brand new females and indoctrinated them into the way we worked. We set up a call centre, a simulated call centre, which went down really well. We also set up a therapeutic community in partnership with a national charity, where the women supported each other through the twelve steps programme whilst coming off drugs and alcohol.

Paige

I never saw a governor, never. Just normal screws. The governor never came on the wing and checked things.

Keith

And the sad thing is, as a governor you can influence so many things, but as soon as you move on, it all collapses. And governors move a lot. I'd been in that prison six years and the opportunity to manage another prison came up, in a totally different part of the United Kingdom. I left in 2001 and within a month they'd closed the therapeutic community down because the area manager thought it too expensive. David Ramsbotham, the Chief Inspector, didn't like the way governors were moved around so frequently; he said you should be there five years minimum, so you can establish your ethos and plan a long term strategy. Governors were encouraged to move every two or three years, it was about developing your own career by working in different establishments. But the prison service had to pay expenses and removal costs, and they're so rigid with budgets nowadays, they're loathe to do that.

Adele

I've always found governors on all levels approachable and helpful. I've had cause to speak to a few over the years on matters troubling me and they've always given me time and good advice. You don't see the number one governor, or any of the governors, around as much as you used to, but I still believe they're approachable and have time for staff.

Keith

Just before he resigned, David Cameron said he wanted to give governors more autonomy on what happens in their prisons and with their budgets. But if you give people responsibility, you've got to give them resources as well, and I'm worried they'll have more responsibility but the budgets won't be sufficient to cope. When Derek Lewis became Director Chairman of the Prison Service in the nineties, he came in from outside and started us down the road of managerialism, the whole issue of setting targets. We did a series for the Perrie Lectures a few years ago, under the banner of hitting the target but missing the point. We're measuring things that don't have any impact on changing people's lives. This strive towards managerialism loses sight of the fact we're in a people business.

John

If every governor's got their own standards, their own regimes, there'll be no continuity. If you do six months in a local prison under one governor and his regime, getting education every day, then they transfer you to another one and you're in your cell twenty-three hours a day because that governor is more focused on something else, that can only be upsetting. It's like saying to every school, you can do what you want. My initial prison governors, for the first ten, fifteen years, I would have given them all the power, they'd been officers and worked their way through, they knew tricks, how to get a prisoner to work for you, what was good and what was bad. But governors now, coming in on fast-track promotions, I wouldn't give them anything, I would take stuff away from them and standardise everything.

What do you mean by fast-track governors?

The governor in my prison was a social worker. Some have been psychologists. They do three months on a wing, six months as a senior officer and then they're a governor. It's a ridiculous concept. You're dealing with people here, vulnerable and dangerous people.

Keith

Fast-track governors go through a completely different training process than I did. I worked as an officer for three years, then went on a three year sandwich course. Fast track governors might get a short spell in uniform but the training's not there anymore and the resources aren't either. I have met some fantastic ones but unfortunately, a lot of them see that role as a step to something else, they don't want a career in the prison service.

Craig

I can't recall too much about governors, except that if one turned up on a wing, the screws would ring and warn others he was on the rounds. We could tell just by the sudden actions. The screws normally sat around drinking coffee would suddenly grow a pair of legs and show interest in what we were doing, engaging in friendly banter and suchlike. The governors had more of an effect on the staff than us, we didn't care in the slightest.

Alice

I never had any interaction with governors, apart from occasional whole staff security briefings. There was a real absence of governors apart from that. They don't come in and see what's going on, and I do think there's a failure to liaise and communicate with education. And as enlightened officers would say, if you're working with them, and creating a good dynamic, you've more chance of them doing what you want. I often wondered why governors didn't pick up on that and use it. They don't utilise education in terms of communication at all. They recognise the importance of raising skills in terms of numeracy and literacy being geared to the workplace, but they fail to recognise the importance of education in relation to subjects such as the ones I taught, and in what they can do to a person's self-esteem. There seems to be a view among officers that raising self-esteem equates with getting an arrogant prisoner, and while that can happen, that is not what usually happens.

Keith

The relationship between prisons and the media has hardened in recent years, because we've had people like Chris Grayling (the previous Conservative Justice Secretary) who've banned books coming into prisons and stupid things like that. Governors are more reluctant to talk to the media these days. In the eighties, they were keen to bring media inside, we had concerts in the chapel, we had a radio programme broadcast live. Governors were more maverick and could do these things, there were less constraints on them. But after Derek Lewis, things changed. We have a press and public relations office in London that have a veto on everything we want to do. It's this culture of blame, as soon as something goes wrong there has to be someone to blame. That demoralises people, everybody's terrified things will go up the line to people like Chris Grayling and they'll get a kick up the backside. Governors are reluctant to do anything different. Peter Dawson, the governor who set up these Clink restaurants inside prisons, I don't know how he managed it in this day and age, because there are so many restrictions and it works brilliant. Fantastic restaurants, great menu and excellent service. Prisons are part of the community. We've got to ensure people in the community can see what is going on inside them.

John

People at the top of unions in the prison service are gobshites. They're not the intelligentsia of the prison service, they're the gobshites who say, come on, one out, all out, rather than think, hang on a sec, this is what we should do. They're the ones the press interview, and if you keep interviewing bullheads then you're gonna get bullheads opinions, and you're gonna form the opinion we're all like that and we're not. The prison service should be saying, look at what we do, the courses we do, the certificates these guys are coming out with, what other agencies are doing in prison, instead of reinforcing it's all about riots and constant negativity. I've been to coroners courts on four or five occasions when somebody's topped themselves, and it's horrible, but it's always blamed on prison staff. What they don't realise, is that in my ten years as a hospital officer, I must have cut down twenty-five people and saved them, I've found people with slashed wrists on hundreds of occasions and saved them, talked to them, spent the night with them. That's never covered. The one time somebody slips through the net, which is inevitable when you've got a thousand people, and all of a sudden you didn't watch him for twenty-four hours, and the family are slating prison staff. It really annoys me that someone must always be accountable. I wanted to say, hang on, we are good at what we do, but you can't go to the press, and if the press come to you, you'd have to be very very careful about what you were saying. Someone's been done recently for leaking bits of stuff. If somebody came up and asked for an interview, I wouldn't be able to do it. You have to go through the governor and the governor will sit with you or tell you what to say.

Intelligence

Daniel

I never went to healthcare. I'm a fit guy and I was never on drugs. In fact, I never even thought about healthcare until my pal died. He had a pain in his leg. The doctor said, don't worry, and basically told him to fuck off. Then he got stomach aches and pains in his back, so he went again and they kept fobbing him off. This went on for six or seven months. He'd lost loads of weight but they kept sending him back with paracetamol. Next thing you know, he's got cancer of the pancreas and he's having to go for chemotherapy. Then he went for a blood transfusion and never came back, he died. And a few years back, this old feller Mark had a lump in his mouth. The doctor sent him to the dentist. The dentist sent him back to the doctor. It took months for this to happen. Then he had a constant sore throat and was collapsing and crying on the wing, then refusing to move out his pad until they sent him to an outside specialist. He'd been telling them for months he had throat cancer. We surrounded the screws and demanded he see an outside doctor or we'd smash the place up. So after ten months of him being in pain and then not able to eat, they sent him to outside hospital and he had terminal cancer. And they could have operated if they'd seen him earlier. He came back to die on the wing rather than go to the hospital wing. He was next door to me. I had James one side and Mark the other. At half two in the morning, I heard him banging on the wall and moaning. I jumped out of bed, pressed the buzzer and started kicking the door. When a screw came, I said, get to his door now, he's not well, and it took them about forty minutes to unlock his door. In the morning he was gone and I never saw him again, he was dead. They say you've got the same rights as everybody else but you haven't. You can't tell me a person out here would go through all that, backwards and forwards between doctors and dentists, everything taking months. It wouldn't happen. So that's what I think of healthcare. Bags of fucking shit.

Antonio

You never want to get ill in prison. The healthcare is neglectful, not because of the care staff, but because of the prison hierarchy and management making it difficult for national health to have access. There's a dentist in this high security prison with eight hundred prisoners, one fucking dentist. He's allowed in four times a week for six hours a time. You get twenty minutes a session, whether you've got a root canal, a jaw hanging off or an infection. And then it's see you when you're next on the list, it could be a month, it could be six months, it could be a fucking year, I kid you not. I've had friends, good friends, die in prison through lack of decent treatment. I had one friend, he was coughing a lot and everyone knew it, the screws, the lads, get him to the fucking doctor. The doctor sent him to hospital and there was a big fucking hoo-hah because they've got to arrange transport, blah blah blah. The doctor said, you've got a shadow on your lung, we have to investigate it, we need to get you back. Two years fucking later, he still hasn't been back and his cough's terrible. We kicked off. He goes to hospital and they go, sorry mate, you've got two weeks to live, you should have come back earlier, we could have cured you. He died in his cell. They asked him if he wanted to go to the prison hospital, but that's another phrase for paedophile wing or insane wing, it's people who are cutting themselves up or want to hide. There's no palliative care, none whatsoever, and the sentences they're giving out, the age of prisoners now, you know there are many men dying in similar circumstances. All they gave him was one of them spongy mattresses, and they said we could sit in his cell with him when we were on association. He didn't get any extra visits or anything.

Keith

People are getting locked up with longer and longer sentences. There's so many elderly prisoners, there's a crisis looming, in terms of health. When you look at the statistics of people who've died in prison, the vast majority are elderly and have died of natural causes, so we need to change the way prisons operate, we need a regime that can deal with that population.

Stephen

People say healthcare is variable and often terrible across the prison system. I say, look at the NHS and it's postcode lottery debate. This isn't a distinctive feature of prisons, it's how we organise healthcare in this country.

Daniel

Two of my pals died and both had about two years left. Yes, they were drug dealers, but did they deserve to die? I don't think so. Was it healthcare's fault? Course it was. Could it have been avoided if so-called professional people had done their jobs properly? Yes. But what happens? The usual prison service cover up. Hide things and don't tell the truth, brush it under the carpet and hope it goes away. And most of the time it does. And prisons do that all the time, with that big phrase 'security intelligence.' They love that phrase, because then they don't have to give you a reason. When I got locked up on this sentence, my sister was a prison officer in a different prison. I had a phone in my cell because it's a private prison, so I'm allowed it, it's not a smuggled mobile. I've just been sentenced to fourteen years so my head's up my arse. I rang my sister up and asked her to ring Tony. She rang him on her mobile, put him on loudspeaker and held the two phones together. I said, Tony, have you got that money? He said, yeah, what do you want me to do with it? I said, give it to my sister. Now that money was from selling my car. When I knew I was going down, I didn't want my car sitting on the drive because it would be worth nothing when I got out. That money was legitimate from selling my car. My sister was giving it to my dad to put in shares. Now I've never been arrested for drugs in my life, I'm in jail for violence, but they pulled my sister into the office, said she was collecting drug money for her brother and suspended her. She said, my brother's not in jail for drugs. It doesn't matter, we've had intelligence. Well, what's the intelligence? We can't tell you because it's intelligence.

Keith

I remember the bad old days of the eighties, when we recruited our own doctors. Some of them were paid buttons and obviously couldn't get a job in the health service. When AIDS became an issue, we had a doctor who wouldn't enter the cell of anyone HIV positive, they'd put a long table in the cell door, with the prisoner at one end and the doctor at the other. Staff would wear white suits and masks when they were bringing someone in who was HIV positive. There was an unbelievable lack of knowledge about how you acquired the illness. But the NHS became involved in the late nineties, when we started tendering the healthcare contracts. And we do have a lot of private companies involved, but the NHS are still funding and as long as they keep a good scrutiny on what's happening, I'm sure we'll meet the relevant standards. There's been a vast improvement, particularly with mental health.

Daniel

Your phone calls are recorded, all of them, in all prisons. Everybody's under random listening and fifteen percent is standard. But I got my security file and 92.3 percent of my phone calls were listened to whilst I was in that prison, and the excuse they gave was that they knew my sister was a prison officer. So my sister went to a tribunal at HMP and they got this big-shot governor to come and sort it all out. But this governor is best pals with the governor at the jail I'm in, so my sister got the sack after nine years, having received an award from the Queen for saving another prison officer's life, after saving two prisoners lives as well. This big-shot governor took over at a high security prison the last week of November. The second week of December, I'm transferred to his high security prison and they won't tell me why because it's security intelligence. I paid for my security file, which you're entitled to, and almost every word was blacked out. I said, what's the point of having my security file then? And the security officer said, there is no point, it's cost you twenty quid for nothing, everyone's comes back blacked out. So I got moved to a Cat A high security prison, even though I was Cat B and hadn't been in any bother in my current jail. And I got moved as a punishment, one hundred percent, because the two governors were mates and weren't happy my sister got the sack and had another job to go to and wasn't that bothered. It's not a coincidence. One governor sacks my sister, then moves to high security as a number one, and two weeks later I'm moved there, two hundred miles from my house, and it's a high security establishment and I'm not a high security prisoner.

Keith

I was working at Headquarters when the story of shipping prisoners around hit the news and we were horrified. It's not something you expect prison governors to be involved in, they're generally a far more honest group of individuals. We did have a thing called ghosting, moving high profile prisoners around because they'd outgrown the place they were in, I met Charlie Bronson after he'd been moved for taking a teacher hostage. There's usually a very good reason why somebody is moved on, they're not moved because the prison's fed up with them. And we don't actually move prisoners anymore, there's a transport contract that the likes of Group 4 have, and they're expensive. The service has been looking at trying to get prisoners back to their home areas, but we haven't got prisons in the right places. The North East of England for example, that area's a net importer of offenders, they've got prisoners from all over the country when they should be back in their home area.

Alice

It is like doing time in one way. There's all the classroom stuff I love, then everything else I detested, and increasingly so, because the prison became so security conscious, and there's far too much pressure on teachers. Security filters down into all departments, into education, its management, and they start to gear everything they do towards security, so managers become prey to the system, they take it out on you and suck you dry. They're like vampires draining the life out of teaching, draining the life out of any rapport with students. And while everyone has to be security conscious and aware, it got to a ridiculous point.

Daniel

And another thing. When I was B Cat, I wanted my C Cat, but they never gave it me because of security intelligence. I wanted a job and they wouldn't let me have it because of security intelligence. I said to the security governor, look, if you've got a problem with me, you need to tell me, because I could be doing something without knowing. It's like if you keep doing something and I say, Richard, you're fucking pissing me off, I'm going to punch you in a minute if you carry on, and you say, what am I doing wrong? And I say, I'm not telling you. Then, two minutes later, I say, do it one more time and I'll fucking punch you, but I still won't tell you what it is. It doesn't make fucking sense. Every security department in every prison does things, and when they're in the wrong, they say it's intelligence, because nobody can question intelligence. I admit security have to do a job, and they have to do it the way they do it, and intelligence does have to play a part in that, but I tell you now, forty percent of the time, they're using intelligence to get rid of somebody because their face doesn't fit, or they're not performing how they want to perform, or they want to fuck somebody over. And you get moved without any notice, they come and get you and you're gone the same day, it's horrible. You never know whether you'll be going every day. Your face doesn't fit. You've said something they don't like. They want to make room for somebody else. Governors doing a one-to-one swap. They're thick as thieves, all of them. I've no respect for anybody in security departments. I've seen really good prison officers become security officers and turn into dickheads, it goes to their heads.

Benchmarked

Sarah

We had four officers on each wing when we first opened, with ninety-five prisoners. Then the cutbacks came. Since 2012 there's just two of us. Morale is terrible. Loads of people left because there isn't the back-up anymore. Years ago, you'd call a response and a hundred officers would come, the wing would be banged up, the situation de-escalated within minutes. Now, you get on the radio and two people turn up, it's frightening. And because we're privatised we can't have a union, we can't go on strike or work to rule, you just have to get on with it. But the prisoners could see there was only two officers, so violence got worse, drugs got worse, it's inevitable. For the first fifteen years I loved it, but in the end, I didn't want to get out of bed, there was no back-up, people were phoning in sick and there was no cover. The prisoners are running that prison now, not staff. Staff have no control over what's happening on the wing, there's no staff on visits, no staff on security. They get phones in, drugs in. Every possible thing has escalated. Probably ninety percent of the wing have mobile phones, and the drugs are terrible, especially Spice, there's people overdosing, ambulances getting called, it's like getting a bag of sweets from the canteen. You still get cannabis and heroin, but everybody's on Spice now, it's blatant. They don't even wait until bang-up, they smoke drugs and get a mobile phone out on the wing, it's unbelievable.

Keith

A few years back we had 134 prisons. They've been steadily closing them and concentrating on the newer prisons. There's probably 110 now, and about ten percent of those are private. And the prison service is a political football. Every time we change government, there's a change in how they view prisons. What we're going through at the moment, with benchmarking, with assaults and suicides, the way Probation has been privatised with Community Rehabilitation Companies, I find it horrifying. I'm still involved with colleagues in the prison service, I'm in London tomorrow for the Perrie Lectures. And some of the stories you hear ... benchmarking has ruined rehabilitation, it's all about warehousing again.

Stephen

There was a recent statement by the National Offender Management Service saying we've had the highest number of women prisoners taking their own lives in 2016, and they attribute this to some extent to lower staffing levels. But there were high numbers of women taking their own lives in 2003 and 2004, when there were much higher staffing levels, so it's not solely a function of that. I'm not saying there isn't an issue with staffing levels, but I am saying those arguments are convenient sometimes. The narrative goes like this: we have hardworking staff, we don't have enough of them, and if only we did, things would be much better. There's a lot more to it than that. Like any groups of staff, some are hardworking and some are bone idle. And with prevailing orthodoxies, it's difficult for other voices to be heard; hence this announcement by Liz Truss to have an extra 2,500 prison officers. It wasn't 2,500 extra teachers or healthcare practitioners. Politically, I can see the appeal of that, but in terms of prisoner care and wellbeing, I'm not persuaded that, by itself, will make a difference.

Daniel

HMP prisons are more stable than private ones. It's more structured in HMP, you can't get away with the same things, because they're on more money as wages, and they're there because they want a career, and there's more prison officers. Plus, it's run by the government, so it needs to be hitting certain marks doesn't it? Whereas private prisons don't give a fuck, honest, they don't care. Private prisons are the best thing that's ever happened to prisoners, one hundred percent. Imagine, when I was fifteen and went to jail, if you'd said to me, in the future, you'll have Sky television and a phone in your cell, not a mobile, a prison phone you can use twenty-four hours a day as long as you've got money on it. You'll be able to go to the gym once a day, have visits where you can walk in a park with your family. I'd have turned around and asked if you were mad. It's only private prisons that have done that, and I got those things because it was my right, not because I manipulated anyone. That's why people in HMP kick off, then go down the block for a bit, just to get themselves into a private nick. It's worse for prison staff though, because they haven't the numbers if anything kicks off. I refused to get banged up once, they pressed the bell and Jesus, four officers turned up. I laughed and said, you four? How are you going to get me in my pad? They said, go in your cell and we'll put a fiver on your phone. I was down the block at the time, and I had a phone and a telly, and they put a fiver on my phone to get me back inside. And they did that because they knew I would have knocked two or three of them out.

John

Prisons have changed dramatically because of the cuts. Courses we were providing; induction, drug courses, classroom courses, they've all been sifted away and now all the prison officers do is unlock, send them to work, wait for them to come back and lock them up again. There's no one-to-one input anymore, and that's what I liked. I could sit with a con and have a laugh, a game of pool when they're on association. You can break down this massive barrier. They called it dynamic security, you'd be finding things out when you were playing pool. That option doesn't exist anymore. By the time you've unlocked the sixtieth cell, you're back locking the first one up. Two years ago, on association, there'd be one officer in the wing office, two on each wing and one floating. Now it's nobody in the office and one on each wing, it's gone from eight staff to three. You can't be spending time talking to one prisoner because there's ninety-four other prisoners wandering around doing what prisoners do. The rapport with prisoners isn't there anymore, and ghettos maybe isn't the word, but if you don't have time to check the four end cells, you don't know what they're up to.

Stephen

I've looked at prison records from 1978 to 2014 and there has been an upwards trajectory of self-harm and suicide. And staffing levels may be an issue, but it's not the driver, because during that time they've gone up and down. What's more important is what staff do, and although there will be critical thresholds of staff levels needed, simply getting more staff in, as the union recommends, won't see suicide and self-harm reduce. Rather than recruit 2,500 prison officers, I'd recruit 2,500 allied health professionals, that would be my approach. I don't see it as a helpful approach to put more prison officers in. I don't see care and control as mutually exclusive categories in the way they're presented. If we care about others, we're more likely to listen to them and do what they want.

Keith

When Ian Dunbar wrote 'A Sense of Direction' in 1995, it was because warehousing wasn't doing anything positive with offenders, and we've got some really good academic thinkers at the moment, who are arguing the way forward has to be focusing on the positive attributes of offenders, on enhancing and reinforcing those instead of being punitive all the time. It's been demonstrated punitive measures don't work.

Sarah

Nobody told us why we were losing officers. Nobody explained things to us. We were never in touch with other privatised prisons. You just worked things out for yourself. Training was done at HMP prisons at first, but now, to save money, they do it at the prison gymnasium. Everything's about making money. We were audited and given eighteen months to turn it around or we'd lose the contract to HMP, so they must have pulled it back a little. But when the Prison Inspectorate come in, they have four officers on the wing, it's all very sly. After they've gone, it's back to two. At lunch time, one officer goes for the trolley and you're on your own on the wing. Imagine something kicking off? You don't stand a chance. Now they're employing young kids, eighteen, nineteen year olds, who have nothing about them, no life skills, who are easily influenced to bring phones in, drugs in, money in, whatever. And that's the sort of people they're employing, because in twenty years, anybody who was any good and wanted a job in that prison has been and gone. It's got that ridiculous with staff, you never get regulars on the wing now, you get people who work in healthcare come and help you for two hours. You're left on the wing with no radio, people in your face saying they're gonna do this and that to you. Honestly, it's unbelievable. And some of these lifers have nothing to lose, they could take you in their cell, never to be seen again.

Keith

There's always that fresh paint issue when the Queen's visiting, you try and put on your best front. But the Inspectorate do unannounced visits these days and that's probably a good thing. As a governor, I grumbled about some of the things they picked up, because sometimes it was a one-off they'd discovered. But they've got a place and I prefer the Inspectorate approach than the previous prison standards from the prison authority, because some of those standards were silly, they didn't have any real meaning. The Inspectorate take a much more balanced view and are there to help you. When I first governed a male prison, the Inspectorate got there before me and produced a report that had 178 recommendations, all quite sensible. My task was to implement them. Some of them were linked to money and I managed to get £3 million to build a new wing.

Daniel

There's no protection for staff in local prisons nowadays, especially private ones. There was two prison officers to ninety prisoners, they've got no control. We're talking four wings and eight prison officers for nearly four hundred prisoners, and this is happening now with private prisons. Prison officers in high security loved me because I walked onto the wing with my England shirt on, I blasted the national anthem when the rugby or football was on, I hated most the Muslims. That was the mentality of that prison. In the private prison, the officers were shit scared of me, because I'm from their neck of the woods and they knew what I was in jail for and who my pals were, and they knew I could make a phone call on a mobile if they did anything to me. It gives you a green light to tread carefully, not take the piss too much, but live a bit more comfortably. And Chris Grayling, what he was doing to jails, saying you're not allowed this or that, you're not allowed to put private cash on your phone anymore, all he's doing is creating people like me to bully others and say, right, I'm putting fifty quid on your phone this week, I'm on standard and only allowed twenty, but you're enhanced. And I'm not allowed to cook my own food anymore, so I want your fucking pudding every day. It just creates bullying when people change things, because prisoners will find a way, and the people at the top of the food chain will always be alright, and all the little fraggles and bully victims will always be little fraggles and bully victims.

Adele

We were benchmarked to see how little we could run on, so we wouldn't be privatised. They call it fence-funding. There's one prison officer for a whole building of classrooms now, including the library next door. That's one prison officer for eighty-four prisoners, and there's eleven teachers there and they're nearly all female. I rang the bell a couple of times and the officers went the wrong way, they went down the old education building. Some officers are fantastic though, they'll patrol and put their head in, ask if everything's okay. Others will stay on the phone, it depends who you're getting. One time, when I was covering a workshop, the lads had been difficult all afternoon. Three tools were missing. I said, it's not happening, I want these tools in, otherwise, when you leave, I'll get you all searched and they'll probably find worse in your pockets. But they wouldn't, and because I'd said it, I had to follow it through. I said to the officer, can you get these last, I want them searched, and he looked at me as if to say, really? But he couldn't search them immediately because he was on his own, he needed a patrolling officer to help. All the other workshops and classes left at five, and it was canteen night so the lads weren't happy. I said, I don't care if they're thrown under the table, if they appear you can go. But our tea's going to be cold, they said, we're going to miss canteen, I've got a phone call to make. I was completely on my own with them, the officer had moved the other classrooms and left. Then a teacher came and asked for a word. He said, you're not going to believe this, but the whole compound's empty, movement's finished and there's nobody here, he's forgotten about you. I said, I've got twelve prisoners, I've got scissors and other tools, he hasn't even done the tool check. And the prisoners were getting agitated. Main education got onto the control room, who got onto the gate. The shift had finished and the officer was on his way home. It was half past five when two officers came over and they didn't have to say anything, they just looked at my face. As the lads went out, I picked up the scissors and said, I'll put these away then. I didn't even get an apology, I got nothing. Our education manager is this big burly bloke who doesn't teach and probably wouldn't feel intimidated anyway. I said to him, I need something done about this. He said, it's not for us to know what Security is doing, it will be dealt with. I requested a meeting with the Security Governor, and he said the same. It basically wasn't my business, as a civilian worker, to know how they dealt with it. That whole story just shows you how complacent they are in there now.

John

If you take wages and meaningful work away from officers, then you're not going to attract quality staff, you're going to get staff who don't have morals. It's going to be a transient job, it is already. People don't get a prison officer's job and work 'til they're sixty anymore; people do five or six years and get out. It used to be a career with a pension at the end, but the pension's garbage now and the conditions are rubbish. The quality of staff is reducing further, it's going back to the Victorian era of bobbies and thugs. If you're capable of doing something else, then do something else. Anybody can unlock a door. Monkeys can open and close doors. If you're not involving them in important things, why would someone go into a job like that? If you're doing seven fourteen-hour nightshifts in a row, it's demoralising, or twelve-hour shifts with no breaks. It wasn't a pleasant job, but it was meaningful and I got something out of it. It's not like that anymore, and it's getting worse.

Stephen

My experience in government is that politicians are only interested in evidence when it supports their own ideology, and there aren't perceived to be votes in looking after prisoners. Part of the problem is that prisons are a public service, and just as the private sector is driven by markets, the public sector is driven by politics. And so the Secretary of State for Justice always has a difficult hand, because other ministers have what are perceived as more worthy briefs.

Keith

Benchmarking is saving money and reducing budgets, nothing else. We're bringing everything down to the lowest common denominator. I worked in Headquarters for the last three years of my service, tendering the Learning and Skills contract, so I visited lots of private prisons, and the worrying thing there is the staff to prisoner ratios are so low, there's no interaction. And calling prisoners by their first names is often a complete no-no in male prisons. Martin Narey, when he was Director General, encouraged us to treat people like human beings, but some staff find that very difficult. But you need to have relationship between staff and prisoners, and there's absolutely no reason why you shouldn't respect offenders. That's what keeps prisons stable, otherwise the whole thing falls down. And we often ignore the powerful influence that staff have on keeping the whole environment balanced. As for the recent government statement about providing £14 million to recruit four hundred new officers, well it's a drop in the ocean, I was running prisons with that budget. The recruiting is going on at an ever frenetic pace, there's loads of courses, but there's a fantastic dropout rate because people go through the training and don't reach the standards they're looking for. And it doesn't help the likes of London prisons, where they have great difficulty recruiting in the first place. They can't fill vacancies because there's so much competition with the likes of the Metropolitan Police Force with their much bigger salary.

Peter

The service I joined said my role was to be the human and compassionate face of the criminal justice system, and my task was to balance the needs of justice alongside the welfare needs of the individual. Now the service I joined was confused over which should take precedence, but would at least recognise that a lot of the time the best way to manage risk and meet the needs of justice, is actually to address the welfare needs of the individual. We've lost sight of the notion of individuals, and the recognition that if you don't accord someone some sense of individual dignity they will tend to behave and respond to you in an undignified way. So the service I joined was quite right on, but the service I'm part of today is not. There's been a lot of erosion of those values, in service delivery and especially in employment and recruitment. Nobody will say that. Nobody will say we're no longer committed to excellence. Nobody will say we're no longer committed to providing the best service we can, to courts or institutions, or to the individuals we're entrusted to work with on behalf of the community. But we're into expedience. We're into the shortest distance. We're into paying lip service. I don't want to sound bitter, twisted and cynical but sometimes I am. I'm very disappointed with the leadership of the Probation Service. I feel hugely let down over Chris Grayling's dismantling of rehabilitation, and absolute horror at the erosion of values.

Caroline

Why try and fix something that's not broken? Probation Officers who've been transferred to private Community Rehabilitation Companies (CRC) from the National Probation Service, their wages are protected but only for two years. And I know it shouldn't be about money but it does matter, and a lot of people will leave if their salaries get affected. Then who are they going to employ? They've already trained people, it's a mess. And low risk offenders that CRC now deal with, they can be really chaotic. They're low risk, high need. They're the people that can't deal with the complexities of life. High risk offenders, those that the National Probation Service have kept, they often have phenomenal skills.

Stephen

I don't understand the logic of privatising probation, cutting it up so the private sector deal with one part and the public sector the other. It's like the NHS; we have Foundation Trusts, which got their status on the basis of being business focused and financially astute, and I'm not sure if there's one in the country that's not in deficit. Commissioning is nonsense. All it does is add cost.

Donna

We worked with individuals. Then they brought in loads of cognitive programmes, where you had to sit down with a script and no deviation, and it might have worked in some cases, but Jesus you could train a monkey to tick a box. You've got to think outside the box, that's when you know what's going on and what to work with. That's what fires me up about working with people; getting in their head, that's how you reduce risk and change people's lives. You try and find them work, you try and find them accommodation, you give them self-respect, you help them. But all that was stopped, and now they've split Probation up, so private companies do low to medium risk and the

National Probation Service stick with high. But what they seem to have forgotten is that medium risk are the ones who have chaotic lifestyles, they're the drug users and child protection cases. So Probation does your high risk monitoring alongside MAPPA, while the poor sods in the private sector, and a lot of them aren't qualified, have all the rest. And medium risk offenders are much harder to deal with and much more volatile, and they're under the radar now, because anything under twelve months, Probation don't have anything to do with them. They're the ones who repeatedly offend, who go into prison, make contacts, come out with no accommodation and go back in again.

Peter

We're bringing in people who are twenty one, twenty two, who've got very little life experience, and a significant amount of them are bitter and twisted within a year of qualifying, it's horrible. The terminology they use to describe people is distressing, I would have been disciplined if I'd used that. At least put ten years in before you get cynical. But they bring people in so much earlier because of numbers. It's the hole in the local government superannuation scheme.

What do you mean by that?

The potential outgoings of local governments pension schemes, by more than a third, exceeds the value of what's in it. So it's to our advantage to have people coming into it and paying into it for a longer time, or to put it differently, paying into it and there being some distance before they're claiming out of it, just because it eases that transition.

Caroline

There's so much pressure on Probation staff to justify the work they do, and yes you should be accountable, but there's a massive difference between that and constantly having to justify what you're doing. If you know you're doing your job properly you can be accountable, but having to constantly write down, this is what I'm doing and this is why, it wears people down, especially when you're working with dangerous people. They've completely devalued the staff that have gone over to CRC. When it was all Probation you had a more balanced caseload. Some were chaotic but others you did structured work with. Taking that away from people is totally devaluing what they're about and why they've decided to do that job in the first place. It's taking away the ability for them to have some kind of emotional reward from work, and if you do that to staff, then they won't perform or want to perform as well, and they'll think, sod it, why am I slogging my guts out for nothing? And if you devalue people they're not supportive of each other, so you no longer feel safe in your working environment and that's scary. That's the private side of things, and it's really sad because it was a system that, on the whole, worked. They dismantled something that didn't need dismantling and that's very short sighted. Yes, there were problems and glitches, but on the whole it was a good system.

Donna

I've been to a few private prisons and it's ridiculous, the whole set-up is about being cost-effective. They shut Young Offenders Institutes down because they said there was a reduction in crime by young people, but some of these YOI's were fabulous, and they kept places that were shit-holes like Wetherby, and then didn't put money into other places for young people with the money they'd saved. Try and give young ones help because they're children, then you might not have problems further down the line. And how can you privatise a service like Probation? Who's the customer? The people making the decisions haven't a clue. How can you palm off your low to medium risk and say our service will have nothing to do with you? And if you want to move this person from medium to high risk, you have to complete a twenty-four page assessment. I had this secretary who now works with medium risk. She says they don't have offices any more, they don't have their own desk, they hot-desk in this industrial estate with a laptop and see people in what they call hubs, Salvation Army and places like that. They go in two's for fear of risk. Jesus, I had to have the safety of

an officer with a buzzer because I was addressing difficult subjects, bu
I was there to address risk. National Probation Service Officers don't
have any real work now, that's all MAPPA ran. They don't do home
visits, one-to-one work, it's just monitoring. And how can you leave
this huge section out completely; the person's family? Nobody works
with the family anymore, they just have to sort things out themselves.

Rebecca

Her smile is warm but nervous. I follow Rebecca into her living room and take a seat. Her son Nathan was sentenced to twenty-five years for the attempted murder of a police officer, and was released nine months ago, having served fifteen years. She also has two other sons who've been in prison. I ask her to tell me about herself, and she speaks softly, and slowly.

I was born in Trinidad and Tobago. My parents are from St Vincent. My mum left me in Trinidad with a lady called Edith and went back to St Vincent. She sent me dresses and stuff, and then wrote to say she was coming for me. I was eight years old when we came to England in 1969.

She puts her head down and presses fingers towards her eyes, as if pushing back tears or forcing pain away. The way she's sitting, her feet don't reach the ground. She swings them left and right, sniffs a couple of times and continues, her voice a little broken.

She brought me to England with my brothers and sisters. We came by ship and lived in someone else's house and all slept in one bed. Then mum got into nursing and they bought a house. But my parents were strict because I was a girl. They didn't let me out, so I ran away. I was put in care homes and excluded from school, then I ran away from a care home and went to London. I met the dad of my two older boys and we lived in squats. I fell pregnant at seventeen with Errol, then at eighteen with Nathan. Me and their dad split up, and I've got another son Rishi, and three granddaughters and a grandson as well. Nathan, he was a little star when he was young. He was bright, not educationally but he had talent. He wanted to be like Michael Jackson and he was very good at sports.

Sophie

My dad was in prison when I was born. My mum had me at fifteen years old. From the very start of my life, all I've ever known is my dad being in prison. I thought it was normal.

Gary

He's in the porch, waiting for me to arrive. Through to the kitchen we walk, where he makes me a cup of tea before leading me into the dining room. We sit down at the table and talk about work and the weather for five minutes, skirting around the real reason I'm here. His wife says hello and retreats upstairs; she doesn't wish to be part of this. And then Gary starts talking about his son, and now he's be-gun, he hardly pauses for breath.

The justice system is shit. They knocked back Jack's appeal for bail, saying he hadn't learned from his first offence. He was thirteen, and he tried to prevent a police officer getting into his garden to get his friend. That was ten years before. And this was the first time a child of mine had been sentenced to prison. Honestly, I broke down. I was at the court with my other son and his mam, my ex-wife. The solicitor said, it's definitely pot luck on what judge you get, but he told us Jack might not even get jail. And then the judge gave him eight years, and I felt like someone had ripped my heart out.

Rebecca

People say gangs, there wasn't such thing as gangs, they're friends. And if you go out with your friends and something happens, then friends are going to get involved. But when Nathan first got into trou-ble, it was really bad. Him and his brother and friends was meant to have taken some boy to the woods and taken his money and stuff. He was thirteen or something. There might have been trouble before, but that sticks out because they went to a young offenders prison. I went to visit them a few times, but I was young and able to do it. Then he said he was going to London to visit his dad, and I got a phone call saying he'd been arrested for shooting a police officer and was charged with attempted murder. I can't really express what you feel when you hear that. I knew that was big trouble, and I know how the police are, so I was worried because Nathan said he had to go to hospital.

What do you mean, you know how the police are?

When it comes to young black men, the police do take advantage. And since Nathan's had his case against the police, they've never left me alone, they've never left the family alone. I've had incidents with my youngest son Rishi where they've come to the house and asked for him, and he wasn't here so I've said so and shut my door. They started kicking it and tried to push their way into the house. I put in a complaint. They told me, no police officers of that name ever worked at this police station. And them same two police officers, they targeted my youngest son, and he did get into trouble, but little things. I mean, if you're young and you're smoking drugs, you don't want your parents to know. But he got a name, because he's Nathan's brother, and then he done certain things and I can tell you, he got a tag and they would ring the box, and he'd be there, and in the morning the police would come and say he wasn't. They'd arrest him and take him to court. It got to the stage that anywhere Rishi would be, whether wanted or not, he would see the police and take off. I lived on the first floor above some shops, and it was so dangerous, but as soon as the door knocked, he'd think it was the police and he'd be over that balcony. I've had times at six o'clock in the morning, Rishi would ring me. Mum the police have been chasing me, I'm hiding in some bushes. Can you please come and get me? And he'd been in there all night. It's been a nightmare when it comes to the police.

Sophie

I knew from a young age that my dad had done something 'naughty' and that is why he wasn't allowed to be at home with us. But I had a perfect life without him so it didn't really matter so much. I used to enjoy going with my grandma and grandad to visit him. The older I got though, the more angry I became towards him. I didn't understand why he would keep coming out of prison and then get himself in more trouble to go back in there.

Gary

Jack rang me Saturday and said, watch The Voice tonight dad, it's the final. I watch programmes I know he's watching, The Voice, X-Factor, Line of Duty, Homeland. Then we speak on the phone about them, or I e-mail him through the E-Mail a Prisoner scheme for thirty pence, and he gets it the next day. But I also watch programmes about prison, and I read the newspaper reports, and it's upsetting. I worry about Jack every day. My wife won't watch those programmes. One of the documentaries was in this privatised prison when my son was there. People were getting punched and being bullied into taking legal highs. It makes me so angry. The guards were just letting it happen.

Sophie

I used to visit dad all the time when I was little, I can't even count how many prisons I've been to. Sometimes we'd drive for hours to see him. My grandma would always make a nice little packed lunch for us. Then I had to go through loads of security and sniffer dogs just to see my dad for an hour. But I used to be more bothered about the kids play area and the chocolate bar we'd buy from the little café in the visits room.

Gary

I could tell this privatised prison was lackadaisical when I went to visit. You'd see people openly passing drugs. This visitor bought a packet of crisps, opened the top, popped something in and gave the prisoner the packet. He swallowed whatever it was straight away.

There were three officers at the desk, just talking to each other, and two further down on seats. Five of them, not paying any attention. They stopped one lad because him and his girlfriend were necking on and his hands were all over her, but that was it. I was glad he got transferred out of there, and it only happened because he knew one of the officers.

Colin

You're not allowed visitors as Cat A, except your solicitor, until they're security checked and cleared. Initially, my then girlfriend was desperate to see me, but it took them eight weeks to clear her. And they wouldn't give her an open visit, it had to be closed, and she cried for most of it, which made things enormously difficult because I couldn't cuddle her, you were just seeing each other through a screen with a prison officer next to you. And that was when I was still on remand, so I hadn't even been convicted. When I moved to high security she had to be cleared again. Then you're in a large hall, sat around a table. The inmate's seat's a different colour to the rest and you're not allowed to get up and move around or touch your visitors. You can on family days but you need extra clearance for them and I never got it. You do have a quick cuddle, but some officers are quick to warn you and make you sit further away. It's enormously difficult on families and relationships, and very few relationships survive prison, especially longer sentences.

Research says family contact, if it's appropriate, is one of the most important factors in reducing the risk of re-offending.

Yes, but you don't see that in this country, you see the complete opposite, they make things as difficult as possible. And it's not any easier for people who are not Cat A or high risk, they still have visits in the same places under the same conditions, their family members are still subject to the same searching. Even children are searched, and yes they have to safeguard against weapons and drugs coming in, but they still get into prison so it's not working. And people are moved to opposite ends of the country to their family, and it seems like that's done on purpose but it might just be a lack of caring in the system. They isolate people certainly, because they're easier to control. If someone has lots of friends in the neighbourhood they think there's a higher risk of stuff being brought in. I don't think that's necessarily the case though, it just makes family contact more difficult. Things do get smuggled in on family visits, but loads more drugs and phones get smuggled in by prison officers.

Paige

It takes that long to wait your turn and get searched, half your visit's over before it's started. My ex used to come and see me every week, he stuck by me twice, but it broke me every time he left. I didn't have no' one else apart from him because everybody else didn't want to know me. You're allowed one kiss when you go in and one kiss when you leave, and that's it. And the guards are alright when all the visitors are there, but as soon as you leave, and you take your shoes off and get searched, they turn into arseholes again.

Rebecca

Have you received any help Rebecca? I know you had help from the church, but has the system helped you? Have you had any emotional support, or financial support for traveling to see your boys?

No, not at all. Well, I once got help from Associated Prison to visit, but if you've got three children in prison and they pay for you to go and see one, it doesn't work out. They put Nathan right up North, it takes over four hours to drive there. Two of his friends took me, but you don't want to be impeding on people all the time. They said they didn't mind, they wanted to see Nathan, but it got to the stage I didn't want to ask no more. One of the guys is a fireman and the other is an athlete, so they got their stuff to do. I didn't see Nathan for two or three years, the last time maybe four years. And if my son was to die in prison today or tomorrow, what would they say? About two weeks ago, I got a phone call from my oldest son. He said, mum, I've been to hospital, someone's broken my jaw. Someone took a brick and hit him in the face. The prison, they didn't phone me, they didn't say nothing. He was in hospital, I could have gone and seen him. They don't communicate with me. Errol, I have his daughter. The last time I went, I forgot her birth certificate. She's been before, she's six years old and they refused to let her in. I had to take a taxi there and taxi back, because if I go in the bus it takes how long, and the taxi's fifteen pound each way. The taxi driver knew my granddaughter though, so he sat in the waiting room with her, and she's quite sensible so she did her own thing. But some things that are done, you have to ask yourself, have people got a heart? Is this really called for?

Gary

The HMP prison, where Jack was remanded, that was stricter, but he couldn't stay there because it's only for remand and he was sentenced. So they sent him to a prison five hours away, because there wasn't any spaces nearer. That's not fair on the whole family. His grandma can't travel that far, she's not well. But it's my son, I'd travel to the end of the world to see him.

Stephen

We could do lots more to improve family ties. Services are sometimes organised to make things difficult. That's not their intention but that's their impact. Children of prisoners have very significant disadvantages. A father going to prison increases the chance of a son getting involved in the criminal justice system significantly, but we don't do much about it, except provide a nice visitors centre, and often that's done by a third sector organisation. We miss real opportunities of working with prisoners children. In some prisons there isn't any investment. The evidence seems overwhelming that this is a much better use of money than sex offender treatment programmes in high security prisons, because the evidence is that those programmes rarely work.

Val

Prison really was sanctuary. I'd been a carer when I was a kid, and prison was the first time in my life someone said to me, what do you want to do? I said, me? I don't understand. Nobody has ever asked me that before. I went to a Quakers meeting and this lady was so nice I couldn't understand why. I asked the screw, do you think she wants me to do something for her? And the screw said, people like that do exist you know. That was the first time I realised you could actually trust some people. I went to the meeting a few times. You weren't preaching to any God, and you did this meditation thing, you had to be quiet for twenty minutes. I thought they're off their fucking rockers here, but the silence helped, because I had lots of nervous energy I couldn't control. But then they started bringing fucking nonces in so I left. There was arts and crafts in the library though, and that helped. I did cards for the kids, I made CD's where I changed stories and put my kids names in instead. My little girl said she listened to her story every night, she can't read or write, and she laughed every night before bed.

Sophie

My mum and dad split up before I was born, so I don't ever remember my mum being upset over my dad being arrested or in prison. She never stopped me from going to see my dad. He was always in and out of prison and he still is now. He had two more children with another lady when I was four or five and I used to go and see them a lot, as well as my dad. But then they started to grow up and realised he was going to be in and out all the time. One of my brothers was very sensitive about the situation and my other brother just didn't really want to think about him. I've got a five year old sister as well now and my dad has gone back into prison about a year ago. It's not fair. Why have more kids if you can't sort your own life out?

Rebecca

You give officers your ID and wait until they call your number. You put everything in the locker, apart from money you take in, then they take you through locked doors. You get searched, you take your belt and shoes off, you get patted down and they have a dog you go past. Once they said there was a razor blade in Rishi's shoe and refused to let us all in. I said, I've come all this way, I don't care what you say, I'm not leaving here until I see my son. So they let me have a closed visit but they didn't let anyone else in. And come on, why would he be taking a razor blade in? They can get razors in prison anyway, and nobody showed us this razor blade. A closed visit is behind glass, you're in a cubicle and you can't touch them. On an open visit you can buy them something to eat and have a cup of tea and make the visit more homely. Some prisons allow two adults and two children, it varies. You sit and talk for an hour, what seems like twenty minutes. You've got prison officers in there, children, men and women who haven't seen each other for a long time. Some of them have like a hundred tables. When I visit Rishi they have a section for paedophiles, and you're bringing the kids in the same room. Different prisons, different rules, different procedures. You never know what their procedure is for stripping. Sometimes they just pat you down and tell you to open your mouth and you go through, other places you're not allowed shoes, belts, earrings, it's take your hair down, take off your headscarf. And you're going to see your family so you want to look nice. It's dehumanising.

Gary

You go in the waiting room for the first time and think, what am I doing here? You look around and hear people saying their son is in for the fifth time. There's the whole rigmarole of getting ID's, getting searched, getting put into a cattle pen before you see him. Then the hug, that precious thing in life, but you can't hug for long or the officers will come, and you can't show any emotions, you've got to be strong. So on the way out, you see all these people breaking down because they're leaving.

Adele

I teach men now, whereas before it was women. And I'd rather teach women because they're more interesting. Men cut themselves off from their family. I'm in here, what can I do? The women had strong connections and it was all about their kids. They used to visit, and they'd get their hair done and make things in the workshops for them, and they'd be all excited. They kept their ties but the men don't. I did a course called Fathers Inside, to help them become better dads and understand they still had responsibilities. I'd say, you're entitled to ring the school and see how they're doing. You can start a story, you can do a bit, send it off and they can do the next bit. Think of the things you want to say to your child. When they're on a visit, sit with them, don't just put them in the corner with a helper and talk to your partner. The men have this culture of, my lad will never go without, he's got the best trainers and tracksuit. I tell them, kids are not bothered what make they've got on their feet, it's the time you spend with them. You could be in the army now, you could be working on the oil rigs. Write to your kids, they're not going to be five all the time, they're growing up. Be a dad.

Val

The kids think it was all my fault and it probably was. His family never really stopped them coming, they just didn't want to. The two oldest ones don't give a fuck, they went through all my bank books and took all my money. One's a drug addict and in with the gang who got their husband and son to run me over, and the other's bi-polar. You just have to get on with it the best you can. The youngest one, she's autistic and in with mental health. I love her and she loves her mum. She'll always stick by me.

Donna

Working with females was depressing and demanding, they had so many issues. And female prisons felt threatening compared to males, and I felt as if the staff had something to prove, and I don't know what that was about either. You get your butch prisoners trying to be clever, and I'm doing my bit about nothing bothers me, I'm not frightened, but Jesus, I always felt intimidated and not a lot intimidates me. There's always someone kicking off or something simmering in the background, and all those women, they could all be on their periods together. Part of my difficulties were probably because I'm female myself, because they could have the same problems as a bloke but I would take it from my perspective. I would imagine what it would be like leaving my kids. Women are still primary carers aren't they? And a lot of the blokes inside, the women are serving a sentence on the outside, trying to manage with the kids, with the stigma of having someone inside, turning up for visits, being searched and having their baby searched, their nappies taken off them. And then you get the woman inside who has all that taken off her; it's probably just too close to home.

Billy

My mother has a mental illness. She controls us all. She's extremely manipulative and she's always going berserk or threatening to kill herself, and I mean every day. My dad is scared of her, and he's twenty stone. I've seen my mam stab him before. And if I argued with my mam, my dad would always stick up for her, even if he knew she was wrong, because he was scared of the reprisals. They did come and visit a few times but it was annoying, I felt like they'd come to my house uninvited. It was always horrible seeing them go though, knowing they'd be walking the streets free and I'd be going back to my scruffy pad on A wing.

Gary

Jack knows he's done wrong. We all know he's done wrong. But he didn't want to plead guilty to a Section 18. We expected two years at the most. I was so angry for those first two years. I didn't show it at work, I couldn't. My family got the brunt of it. Strangers got the brunt of it. And then you see the victim on TV and in the papers, portraying my son as someone he isn't, and lying about certain things. I went to counselling. The first session I broke down. But they're brilliant and I can see the change in myself. I blamed myself, but they told me it wasn't my fault and that helped massively.

Sophie

My dad has been in and out of prison my whole life, so when he came home for a short period I tried to build a relationship with him, but it never fully worked. We went on a few little holidays in England which was okay, but I would always want a friend with me. Really, I just wanted a normal dad who loved me, but I've never had that.

Adele

The men are in and out and they just don't care. I've seen so many of them, constant offenders and petty thieves. One that did the Fathers Inside course, he had four little girls and they were amazing. We used to have a special visit on the course. But he couldn't take the hassle of having these kids, so he would come in for an eight month rest. He'd do a crime to get out the way. I'd say, they're growing up, don't you think she needs your help? Ah, she'll manage, she's got her mother, I'll see them on a visit. But when you get out, they're going to be a year older and you've missed all this time. Ah, they're alright, they do my head in, all that noise, girls everywhere.

Gary

I saw Jack last weekend and he wanted me to get him a drink from the machine. But there wasn't the one he wanted so he got up and started to walk to the machine and the guards were suddenly all round him. He said, I'm just telling my dad what drink I want. They said, sit down, how do we know you're not about to start a riot? It's ridiculous. But another time, I was waiting to leave after a visit, and this woman came over and said, I'd like to thank your son for looking after my son. Her son was forty year old and my son was twenty-three. My wife started to cry. I started to fill up. This other man owns a pub and they've said, as soon as Jack gets out, they'll offer him a job.

Antonio

I wrote an article for the prisons newspaper, Inside Time. The prison inspectorate were there and some lads on the landing said, can you read this? This inspector took it away and they changed the rules, they made this prison allow prisoners to spend private cash making phone calls. The black market for mobile phones died immediately, mobile phones are not worth a wank in that prison now, and it's the only high security prison with that procedure. Because if my wife wants me to ring her, and she sends me her own fucking money, I should be allowed to maintain family contact. In most prisons that's not allowed, you're on a fiver a week for sewing mail bags, just enough for toothpaste and tobacco. And the private companies charge premium fucking sex line rates to phone your wife and children. So tell me, who's being served by that?

Rebecca

My mum was at death's door, and when she died, they didn't let Nathan come to the funeral. My brother, we bought his suit, his shoes, he was inside the same time, but they never let him come either. The nearest prison said they couldn't keep him overnight, the police station said they wouldn't have him. I thought, if there's one thing they'll let you out of prison for, it's to bury your own mother. Reggie Kray was let out to bury his mother. So why? What are these things meant to do? Are they meant to break us, or bring us to nothing? Even the stuff we sent our brother, the suit and everything, he doesn't know where they've gone, he didn't get them. We've sent money a few times, money never gets there. And that's not just happening to us, other people tell me this. And now you can't send clothes, they've got to work and buy them from the catalogue. My son's been in six months and he's got one set of prison clothes, he's put weight on and he's bursting out his trousers. And even if you can get a job, how long do you have to save up for a pair of trousers, a pair of underpants or socks? So instead of letting them have a telly, why not let them have their own clothes? My son's told me a little bit of what goes on in there. He's seen people die, people commit suicide. Even Nathan now, when he's sleeping, you can't touch him and wake him from his sleep, because when you're in prison you don't know who's going to come and do you something wrong. And for fifteen years, every two hours, someone would come to his cell and switch the light on, so he's never slept through the night once.

Donna

Originally, it was all about keeping contact with the inmate and their family. Then they stopped caring whether you had contact with the family. Then it was reduced time when you went to visit the prisoner, they knocked it down to only going there for sentence planning or parole reports. And that was all prisons and all prisoners, and it's awful, because the only contact they really have, apart from prison officers and probation in there, is us, and if that's time limited you're not developing a relationship you need to have. You're writing a parole report and only taking information from prison staff, you're going off other people's reports and comments, and a report can make a big difference. I had this lifer. You always kept your lifer wherever you or he moved around in the country. I saw him three or four times a year and visited his family. I had him sixteen years and built up a hell of a relationship. When his mam died I had quite a responsibility as a Probation Officer, and when he was in bother, I turned up and had good input. This lad was getting to the end of his sentence, he'd been through high security, ordinary conditions, weekend visits. I went to his home on a weekend and met up with him. Now that's all gone, and it does have an impact on risk to the public and risk to themselves. Now it's all about what looks right, on the assessment. They don't care that this is a person that went in as a young lad, that had one relationship in his life, had lost his mam and had come out as a man that is just meant to get on with things. Nobody gives a damn anymore.

Double Bubble

Colin

To survive, I started a shop. The cheapest thing on the canteen sheet was noodles, so I bought some and started selling them two for three through the week, when people were hungry, and people are always hungry in prison because the food's shit and you don't get enough of it. The noodles were pennies, they were under ten pence, so I got as many as I could, but my wages were less than two quid a week, because I was on enforced bang-up. I gave away two packets but insisted on three back on canteen night. I built that up and added things as I went along, from noodles to chocolate, packets of crisps, biscuits, tobacco, sugar, tea and coffee, toiletries and shower gels. I was putting an ounce of tobacco out for an ounce and a half back. Then I got a deal going with a lad doing pills, he wouldn't allow them pills without tobacco. In the end I was turning over hundreds of pounds a week, but it was all in goods, there's no money. It kept me in food and tobacco and coffee, as much as I wanted.

The prison system doesn't allow that surely; having your own shop?

It's totally against the rules, but they turn a blind eye for the most part. I had prison officers asking me for chocolate and biscuits to have with their tea, so they get freebies from time to time and it keeps them quiet. When I left prison I passed debtors onto friends, as a dropsie. I guess you're trading in people. It probably sounds horrendous but that's what you do.

What was the most anyone ever owed you?

Hundreds. It was beneficial to have people owe you, because they had to buy for you every week and couldn't get out of debt, so you got most of their wages every week. You don't actually get their wages of course, you give them a list and they buy you what's on it. Then you re-stock your shelves. My pad was full. Under the bed there's a cardboard box for properties, that was full of crisps and biscuits. You get a locked cupboard, that was full of tobacco and stuff. Other pads were full of my stuff. You're only allowed a certain amount, so you get other people to store it for you, mainly because they owe you. Sugar was a good one, you could always make money on sugar.

Billy

I used to loan baccy and get double back, all the time. I don't smoke but baccy is currency. I had that much in my pad once I had to spread it across other pads. You're only allowed two or three ounces but I had about ten. If I was hungry, I'd give baccy for food, or if I wanted shower gels. But I didn't need food that much because I worked on the servery in that prison so I got as much food as I wanted.

Craig

I remember reading prisoners have flat screen TV's and all sorts, so I got a shock when I seen this old thing. But you can have a TV and it costs a pound a week, there was that and a kettle. Everything was plastic; plates, trays, mirrors, razors. You have to request toilet roll from the office and if you have the wrong screw on, they say, come back later, knowing you can't do without and taking pleasure from it. If you went to another prisoner, they'd say, I haven't got none spare. Normally, you'd think, you tight bastard, you can't even give us a bit of shit paper, but you learn it's a commodity, sachets of coffee are a com-modity, you get one sachet a day and four sugars. They're only little spoonful things, but if you don't take sugar, you can build them up and swap twenty sugars for two coffees. Money has no meaning whatso-ever. I had money outside, but you never see coins, so sugar, coffee and shit roll become forms of currency. And then you have double bubble. Someone will say, if you're stuck, I'll get you a bar of chocolate, but next week I want two back. It's a popular thing, double bubble.

Paige

It happens all the time. They swap baccy for hair dye. Men's jails is different to women's though, because in men's you're allowed to get razors and that's it, but in women's you have to have ID and then take the razors back after so they can check them, because of all the people self-harming.

Colin

You could eat okay on full-time education or work if you didn't smoke, if you spent all your wages on canteen food. The prison I was in was one of the better paid, you could make fifteen pounds a week if you were on full time education and enhanced, more if you worked. If you smoked, that would leave you a pound a day for food and toiletries, but if you didn't you'd have two pounds a day. If you wanted a balanced diet you had to pay for it, there's very little fruit comes off the servery and it's not good quality. You sometimes get an apple or an orange but they're tiny. You wouldn't expect good quality in a prison though. Who cares what prisoners eat, eh? You're always seen as second quality human beings.

Gary

Jack says some people don't do anything. They get three pounds a week basic and that's it, they don't have anyone sending money in. I send money for his phone card, and he gets on well with others, so he gets things when lads leave, he's just got a pair of trainers off someone. He's got a brand new tracksuit as well, but they won't let him wear it because it's black. You can't wear black because that's the colour officers wear. But he's eating well. He gets money sent in and he's become a qualified barber so he gets things for cutting hair. He does haircuts for a couple of tins of tuna, because he's started the gym again.

Val

I had my own little shop. I've always survived. I gave one chocolate bar out and got two back and it grew into a mountain. The screws knew what I was doing but they didn't care. I didn't smoke, I didn't drink, I didn't even eat chocolate. I did a lottery and a snooker tournament and gave ten bars to the winner. I gave baccy to screws to give people down the block, and I never asked for anything in return. I never went down the block myself, I was too crafty for that. I had tactics and survival instincts, I call them life skills. If you're going to do something then do it, but the best kept secret is the one you keep to yourself, do you know what I mean?

Gary

You've got to be careful when you ask for a cigarette because they might have put Spice in, and it only takes a drag or two. Jack makes sure he gets tobacco rather a rolled cigarette, so he can check it himself.

Colin

The food was horrendous. The menu might look nice in the newspaper but it's disgusting. It improves when the prison inspectorate come along and then it goes back to normal again. You get a cereal pack on an evening, you're meant to keep it for breakfast. It comes in a little tidy-tied plastic bag, a scoop or two of whatever. But your meal at dinner doesn't even touch you, so you end up eating your cereal as well. Lunch is a sandwich with a kids size bag of crisps, like you would put in an infant's schoolbag, except for weekends when you get a cooked dinner. The portion sizes got progressively smaller when I was there, presumably to cut costs, but some of these kids are eighteen stone full of muscle.

Billy

The food was shit. If you didn't work in the servery, you'd be hungry all the time, if you couldn't top up at the canteen. When I got recalled, I couldn't get my job back on the servery. I was fighting and always on basic, so I didn't have money for canteen. Loads of lads from one town were on the servery on my wing. This lad gave me a couple of poxy chips and his pal, stood next to me, had a plate piled high. I said, you can fucking put more chips on there pal. He said, no that's all you get. I said, you're taking the piss, I'm on basic, get my fucking plate filled up now or I'll jump over there and fill it myself. He was like, calm down lad, calm down. They were the bullies of the wing but I didn't care, I was on basic and had nothing to lose. I told him he was a fucking muppet and I'd kill him. He filled my plate up. They were alright after that, they left me alone and put loads on my plate. They even came to my pad and asked if I wanted it mopped out.

Colin

The prison took to baking their own buns. You could brick somebody to death with them. They have a tiny slice of corned beef or cheese in the middle. Dinner's a hot meal usually, chips that have seen better days, very meagre portions to say the least. Some of the stews are very suspect, and because it's VP you're always scared of liquid food because things can be put in there. A portion of fish is a safe meal, but not soup or stew. The food's made in the Mains kitchen, and you hear reports of meals smelling of piss and shit, it does happen. The prison occupies a lot of ground space and it could easily use some for growing vegetables and creating wholesome menus. There'd be no labour costs because plenty of prisoners would love it, but they refused, saying prisoners would hide things in the soil.

Billy

Some kids who got picked on all the time, they got the smallest portions you've ever seen. There is officers there, but they don't care. This

one kid, he'd never done jail in his life and was only in for driving offences. I swear to god, he must have been given three chips, a spoonful
of beans and two little sausages. I picked my sausages off my plate and
gave them to him. I felt bad for loads of kids in there, getting tortured
all the time. How can the screws put up with that?

Learning To Find Your Place

Adele

I initially started doing one afternoon a week, doing book-making with women. It was to give them something to do during the summer holidays when other teachers were off. The sessions were very relaxed. It was a Category A wing and I didn't have keys, I got to the vehicle lock with my box, filled with scissors and wire and God knows what, then someone took me over, put me in the classroom and said, shout when you're ready. I was there for two hours, on my own with the women. But the first woman who walked out the room, women being women, they said, do you know who that was? Do you know what she did? The course ran for three months, until we'd used the last penny of funding. Then a yoga teacher handed his notice in and I took his hours, even though I had no qualifications. I was green really, I had no idea. It was a totally different culture to what I was used to. I'd been working in a cafe, trying to get a massage and acupuncture business off the ground.

Alice

I was a mature student in my early thirties, and I'd wasted a lot of chances, academically. I was studying English but I discovered that I loved Philosophy, which I'd taken as a subsidiary subject in first year, so I very tentatively moved over, and then I was offered a scholarship to do a PhD. I still had dreams of doing other things, and times of not being sure what I wanted, aged forty, but teaching is what I went into because I love passing on things I've learned myself.

Adele

My salon was in this converted cell. I don't know how we managed but we did, the women got their hair and nails and ofen make-up done and that was all that mattered. This high profile lifer, her pad was a couple of doors up. When she was going to court, there'd be supervising officers, prison officers, dedicated search team, dogs, a helicopter overhead. She'd get back and they'd say, just take her in there will you Adele, calm her down, she's in a bit of a state but she's alright with you. I did reiki on her but she wasn't even aware, she'd be ranting and almost foaming at the mouth.

Nigel

I worked at an HMP prison as an officer for a couple of years but decided I wanted a change. So I studied for my PGCE and then went to teach in a women's HMP prison, but after a year there I transferred to a men's high security prison. Altogether, I've had about seven years' experience of working in prisons.

Adele

I got work in a men's prison through a friend I'd been to university with, who was working there. The Head of Education said, someone's just handed their notice in, there's five sessions of English and Maths going. I said, I'm not an English and Maths teacher, and he said, Adele, any teacher is a teacher of Maths and English. This prison's in London, thirty miles away from where I live, but I needed the permanent job. My first class was an English class with sixteen men I'd never met before. I tried to prepare for every eventuality and I know now, I should have just taught one thing. They had my life, it was the longest two hours ever. I had a cardigan on my chair and they tied the sleeves together. Half a dozen of them were saying, come on lads, but they knew I was fresh meat. The boss came in and said, is everything alright? And I said, yeah, it's fine. That was a turning point for me, no lesson was ever going to be that bad again. Now, it doesn't matter how many are in my class, there will always be more that know me than don't. There's a high turnover, but if three go and two come, there's still six or seven that have always been there. And those lads will say, you can't do that in here mate, she'll have you. And if someone winds me up too much, it will be, get out, you're not coming back. But miss. No, get out. I'd get the officer and they clicked, if they don't toe the line they'll get kicked out and won't get paid. Once they knew the ground rules they were alright, I was just too soft before. But that was in the days when you could put them out, and that doesn't happen anymore.

Alice

I initially taught in secondary schools but I hated it. There was a huge number in one classroom, which isn't my forte. Then I worked in a women's prison briefly, covering others teachers, but I found the women really hard to work with, so I moved into the men's high security prison, and I taught there for twelve years. I brought Philosophy into the prison and they loved it. I looked after all the Open University students as well, and that included all the people doing GCSE and A' Level. And if they needed past papers, or this, that and the other, I would go to great lengths to make sure they got what they needed, because it mattered to me. And then I started teaching Critical Thinking.

Stephen

One of the ways to prevent suicide and self-harm in prison, which is not routinely done, is to meaningfully occupy people throughout the day, it's as straightforward as that.

Nigel

I contextualise everything within the classroom. I produce projects that address all aspects of the curriculum and allow for the men to develop hobbies such as bird watching. And they are able to do that in this prison, because the prisoners see a variety of birds. We have oyster catchers, jackdaws, pied wagtails, house martins and swallows, and because of nearby ponds we often see mute swans and Canada geese in flight.

Craig

I went to the library and it was a bit of escapism. You're only allowed ten minutes a week, so you have to know what you're looking for. At first I got books on farming, parrots, cars, I was clinging onto normal life to give us hope. Then I got magazines and saw things like mobile phones. They were out when I was, but there was no smart phones, nothing like that. So I started to watch The Gadget Show, to see what was happening in the outside world. I started education because I wanted to get to the library more and so it was two birds with one stone. I started in art class, I done silk paintings. One was of me in a sunflower field, walking in freedom but still in prison clothes. I didn't get to keep any pictures, I asked the teacher God knows how many times. She said they went on display. I think they're still in there somewhere.

Colin

I grabbed education with both hands and tried to get whatever positive I could. It's a good distraction from what's happening around you on a daily basis, and because it's creative it's filling your imagination and moving you in a positive direction, rather than imagining what's going on outside your door. But it's had its funding cut so you can't go as far anymore. I did GCSE and then A' Level in fine art but I don't think you can do A' Levels now. I've always loved art, I used to do tattoos but I'd never picked up brushes, so I gained that from prison. But the prison kept the pictures and wouldn't give me them back. I asked for them many times, and then, when I got recalled, I asked for them again. They said they'd be at reception when I got released but they weren't. They have a cavalier attitude towards peoples stuff, it doesn't matter because you're just a prisoner. It was enormously disappointing, enormously. All of those hours I've done, through GCSE and A' Level, and I have none of my paintings at all.

Alice

I remember one day. It was when classroom doors had to be kept open because the prison demanded it. Sometimes, as a teacher, you're aware the officers outside can hear what you're saying, and while most of the time that's fine, there were other times you'd feel a little self-conscious, because you do build rapport and you wonder if it will be seen as anti-security, when I knew it wasn't and I could handle my classes. But this particular day, it was an unruly class and they took a lot out of me. I used to dread Thursday afternoons sometimes, because they were so hard to manage, and by that I mean the level of noise. They would get so engrossed in Critical Thinking, asking questions left, right and centre, and these were men who weren't that disciplined in the social skill of not interrupting when others are speaking. At one point I had to go outside to get something and I expressed exasperation at the noise, and the officer said, I have to tell you love, I've been on education nine or ten years, and I've never seen a class so enthusiastic. I said, but they're so noisy, and he said, yeah, but everything they're talking about is Critical Thinking. So that was a real success, impressing an officer in the right way. And Critical Thinking is really important. It can be applied outside the classroom, in ordinary lives; how to use a reasoned best approach. Cognitive Behavioural Therapy within Psychology is part of this.

Billy

English class was my favourite. I used to read all the time, write all the time. I wrote poetry and I was learning to spell better because I was never really in school. I didn't gain much from education though, apart from getting better at spelling and writing. I got Industrial Cleaning qualifications and English and Maths ones. I just went on the cleaning course for something to do though, I'll never use it.

Alice

I only taught local women, and only briefly, and I think I would have gelled better with high security women. There's something about the high security population, their deeper problems, that I feel I can get in there and do something with. I found it hard with the women. A lot of them, maybe all of them, had been dragged up, had been in and out of homes, had parents who were addicts, or they were addicts. They had no social skills, they'd come into the class and everything they did was designed to shock. And the subjects were different; I was covering basic Literacy and Numeracy there. It was much easier for me to work in high security.

Paige

I stayed awake the first few nights, crying and listening to the pipes. Nobody cares about you in there. I was locked in my room for five days until they had space on courses. I did English and Maths. It was alright but some of the prisoners there were little twats. If you couldn't read they'd take the piss out of you. I didn't have time to finish my English and Maths qualifications though. The only one I got was First Aid.

John

I get on with most civilian staff but there's definitely trust issues. Prisoners relate better with civvies and uniformed staff are suspicious because we aren't bright enough to think we've got a uniform and they haven't. And if an officer does nothing but unlock and lock all day, and he sees someone else having meaningful interaction for an hour or two, it's natural he's going to be suspicious and resentful. They started taking our jobs. Drug courses were taken by Drug Action Teams, it was cheaper and the contract made the governor look good, and it was a professional body rather than officers with eight weeks training. You'd be back on a wing, unlocking for dinner. The quality work you were getting rewards for disappeared, and more and more courses and education classes were taken over by civvie staff. They're probably better at it than we are, but we were doing it one day and not the next. And the more civvies that came in, the more defensive we got about our own roles. We didn't want them because then we'd see ourselves purely as turn-keys, and it's demoralising if that's all you're doing.

Alice

Officers are suspicious of teachers. It's part of the whole security consciousness increasing in prison. You are viewed with suspicion, as a negative influence in some way. You have obstacles you really shouldn't have. It's almost like you're colluding with prisoners. I felt tarnished by some officers attitudes, like I had done something wrong.

Craig

After art I did creative writing. I did poems and short stories and then a bigger story and I got to know these characters so much I felt as though they were part of me reality. It's still ongoing and it's up to sixty-six thousand words, but I'm still putting me life together, whereas inside creative writing was a big part of each day. Now life is getting in the way, bills and appointments and this course I do. It's become secondary but it's something I've clung onto as the one good thing I got out of prison. Actually it's not the only good thing, I think prison has done me confidence a lot of good, because now I see rough lads in pubs and I know what they're like beyond the veneer. I say, alright lads, and go through the middle of them to get to the bar. I used to help lads like them. If they had a letter to write, with creative writing and IT, I'd write it down and readjust it, so they weren't waffling on, because these were sometimes letters to solicitors and they would waffle on for four or five pages. I'd read it out to them and they'd be happy and send it off. I've seen the vulnerable side of these lads.

Alice

Maths and English are vitally important, of course they are, but with subjects like Philosophy and Critical Thinking, and others like Creative Writing and Film Studies, students relate the content to their own life experiences. But yes, you have to be careful, because you don't want someone to come up with things they or you can't deal with in a class. I did my PGSE whilst I was teaching inside and one of my tutors came to observe a lesson. I handed her the lesson plan and she told me later, she thought, God, this will never work. The subject was Plato and the Ancient Greeks and the lesson was on platonic love. It had to be thought about and handled carefully and it was, and at the end the tutor said it was probably the best lesson she'd ever witnessed, given the surroundings. The whole notion of love, I related to the different levels of friendship through early childhood right to the current, how they relate to you being recognised by the other, how different levels within you are recognised and validated and how, as your sense of self increases, you get to know yourself better. On the one hand, they're gaining knowledge about the ancient Greek view of friendship and working towards an exam – on Philia, not the Eros that love is often reduced to - but on a psychological level, there's so much more, about themselves, about nurturing. Some of these men looked back through their lives and saw how they'd been deprived from childhood of any good relationships, or they picked out relationships that did have meaning and explored why, and that filled in parts of the jigsaw in terms of self-understanding, which is really important in rehabilitation. And so this woman, who'd hardly ever been into prison, was observing this lesson, with men who'd been imprisoned for being in drugs gangs, for murder, robbery and theft, for serious violence, and they were all wanting to learn. Sure, some of their minds were more open than others, but you could see the others, even grudgingly, beginning to open their minds, and this woman witnessed these big tough men, talking about friendship and love. And what she had come in and panicked about, she went away feeling enriched about.

Adele

Once the lads settle down, most of them do become alright. The one who's going to thieve the most, I give him the pens. Look after those for me will you? Get me twelve in at the end of the day. It works. I used to concentrate too much on the disruptive ones, all lesson it was, please stop doing that, please sit down. Now I overpraise the good ones sitting quiet and the disruptive lads notice. I say, I haven't got time for you today, this lad's working towards an exam. And it works, it really does. Eventually they say, alright then, show me how to do it. Oh, you want me to show you now? Well, I'll be over in a minute, I'll just finish with this lad. They're like petulant children, ignoring negative behaviour works. We had to do our yearly self-assessment today. I've had 737 enrolments and my expected achievement is 89%, I don't think that's too bad. Some of them might have been transferred before they took their exam, so they haven't failed. I'm not sure how, but we're getting somewhere.

Nigel

The women tend to have been beaten, and they're emotional wrecks. There are many hard cases in there too, but the majority, as research indicates, are usually of low education and have been in abusive relationships. The women tend to talk about their circumstances though, whereas men don't.

Val

I found out I was dyslexic in education. I loved learning and they showed me different ways to learn. And education was a scream. I had this little hot water bottle and when the lasses started on me, I'd run down the corridor and smack their arses with it. Or we'd have a song coming on, and it was like The Full Monty, we'd all start clicking our fingers and turn up dancing. And Christmas in there was the best Christmas I've ever had in my life. I put my stocking outside my cell on

Christmas Eve. Nobody else did, just me. Everyone said, you're mad, but I said, no, you've got to believe. I got a chocolate biscuit, some sweeties, quite a lot of stuff because I'd made sure it was the biggest sock I had. Then I showed all the lasses and we played bingo and had a Christmas dinner.

Stephen

It's a common myth that officers spend most time with individual prisoners. There are instructors in workshops and teachers that get to know prisoners a lot better, have a lot more direct contact and have to negotiate some pretty difficult relationships.

Adele

I've never been threatened by any prisoner, I can honestly say that. Once, when I covered a maths class because the teacher was sick, a big fight broke out and five of the girls formed a barrier in front of me. They went, Adele, get behind, get behind. And the bell went and the officers came, and there were tables upturned and everything. Sure, being sworn at, I can't tell you how many times, but if you put it all in the pan and boiled it down, it probably isn't that much.

Nigel

I feel safe in the classroom. The officers are very supportive and I never really need help, just having the learners removed on occasion and even then it's usually the officers telling them they have to leave and they comply. Learners are risk assessed and the prison does its best to ensure your safety.

Alice

There are men I didn't get on with, who gave me a hard time, but not that many. For the most part I had a great response from my students, and my exam results reflected that. I remember one saying, you're the only class I come to, because in here I'm treated like a human being. That was expressed lots of times; being treated like a human being, and education is so linked with self-respect and dignity. If somebody feels these things, you're leading them away from the path of crime, because you can't truly respect yourself and commit crime. You're losing something of yourself when you commit crime.

Antonio

There were several blokes like Wrighty and there was a pattern to it. They came to me more honestly, like look I'm a dickhead, I fucked up, not, do you know who I am? I was more relaxed in their company and they were asking me questions about education and stuff. I taught them how to play chess and I was smashing them, not deliberately trying to beat them up, because that's just ridiculous, but trying to get them to my level by showing what I'm doing and teaching them openings and how to finish quickly. But they sneaked off and got books out the library, then turned up the next weekend with brand new openings and tactics and wiped the fucking board with me, declaring five-nil, six-nil, and then giggling and sniggering. And basically, they'd been away all week, practising these openings, and I'm just wandering around the wing smashed, waiting to have phone calls with my Mrs, not even thinking about fucking chess. Then they've followed me through the educational path and done much better than me, and I'm dead proud of them. They've gone behind their doors, sent off for courses, done their ABC's, struggled through the education system because it only goes up to level 3, then applied, with my assistance and others, to outside bodies to get funding for degrees and so on. Some of them have reached educational goals that outside take three years and have taken seven fucking years inside. Education stopped Open University classes because they weren't making money for the college, you had to do it in your pad. You have to write five thousand word essays by hand, and write them four or five times because they have to be legible and you get marked down for spelling mistakes. And you've got to put references in and if the reference is wrong you can't cross it out, you've got to write the whole fucking page again by hand.

Alice

Rehabilitation and reintegration into society are often overlooked; subjects where you're teaching skills about being a person interacting among other people. It's not all about how to work a machine. I've seen within the prison system, men who came in with little more than basic skills, who years later have gone on to Open University and Post Graduate study, and the concomitant change in their personality and emotional health, and view of their past life, all went hand in hand. They had a much more mature outlook. I'm not saying all psychological quirks were taken away and cured, but a lot of them were able to heal themselves in some ways.

Antonio

That high security prison is a force against bettering yourself educationally. Most of the lads are only in there because of lack of education, lack of knowledge, a lack of looking around and working out what the fuck is going on, which are the tools of education when you think about it, whether you're learning English, Maths, Chemistry, whatever. What you're really doing is looking at something, digesting it and telling someone about it, to show you understand what the fuck's going on. It's just multiple thinking processes. You're learning to find your place on the planet, look at history books and see why the fuck you're there, and maybe work out what's going on with this emotional turmoil you've been born with. But in my experience, prison was a dark force against the good of education, a deliberately, malignantly, heartless fucking against any endeavour to educate yourself. They stopped books for fucking years. I educated myself despite the system, and I'll give you one glaring example of the shambles I was up against. I spent two years doing English Literature A level, two fucking years. I did all the course work and the exam, and I think I did well, but there was a large turnover of teaching staff and my teacher was poorly and didn't put the fucking exam in. Then she turns back up and she's lost the exam paper and not even fucking registered me. Two years of my life, sitting in her class. And she can't teach, you'd see the top of her head, she'd give you the book and it was crack on son. Me and Wrighty used to work through it together, and when we asked her anything, she didn't have a fucking clue. At first, there were education staff who were keen as fuck and they flew me through GCSE's, then it came to A' levels and they became thin on the ground. I got an A star in Art though and was dead proud of it, and that allowed me to approach the authorities for funding to take education further, and then it was all by mail to the Open University. But that was even more of a shambles. I had an Open University manager inside the prison and she kept me paying for these modules year after year. Then one year, as I was getting out, I thought I wonder how many points I've got, how many I need for my degree. I fucking looked and I'm only sixty points, eighty points over what I needed, and I've just done an unnecessary module. I didn't even get a graduation. I had to kick off just to get the fucking certificate to say I had a degree.

Alice

Ofsted don't help create better education. The education department, and it's probably no different in schools, dress everything up for the inspection, because they have prior warning. Our education department did very well, but did the prison utilise that? So what was the point? It's not like you have parents, coming with their kids and saying, we'd like this prison rather than the other, they have a higher Ofsted rating. Fair enough, if a prison education is below standard, they've got to bring the standards up, but the education department is seen as this little hub within a prison, that's separate from everything else, it's the civilian block within a regimented regime, it's 'we've got to keep that lot on par with us, doing what we want.' The relationship shouldn't be like that, it should be working in tandem, utilising what the educators are doing, liaising with them, getting it to work for the prison and the prisoners benefit, in terms of rehabilitation and having a more content and less aggressive prison population. On all levels, there's a failure there. You hear the odd voice within Psychology, or the odd governor, asserting something about utilising the education system more and more, but it never happens.

Adele

I don't go into work every day thinking I'm under threat, even though I was left in the education block with twelve prisoners, but I know for a fact, because I've been told, that if something was to happen, it would be cheaper for the governor to pay out compensation than provide protection to stop it happening. There's simply not the money. They look at figures instead of people. There's only three workshops out of ten running now, because in education alone we've had twenty-seven staff leave in one year, and fifteen of those were workshop. And rather than men being put into classes they should be in, they put them in wherever there's a space. So they go into induction and it all looks great on paper, they have an interview with the national careers service and are told, these are your options, what do you want to do? Nine times out of ten they'll want workshops, waste management or a cleaner job, none of them will mention English, Maths or IT. But because those classes are the only ones they don't need extra security checks for, whereas they do for workshops because of the tools, and the governor wants them all out their pads doing purposeful activities, they turn up at the class and say, I didn't put down for this. The prison's created some words for it. You have to say, this is a 'pathway' because English and Maths will help you in the workshops, so you're in here until a space becomes available. And it very rarely does, because they haven't time to check, and new people come in and if there's a space, they get it. Then our men get disgruntled and kick off and you end up putting them out. You spend your whole lunch doing Information Reports, because you can't get them out of your class unless they've had three of them, and so you have to suffer them in the meantime. And if you do get them out, they're only out for two weeks and then they're back and nothing's changed.

Alice

The VP's are much easier to manage because many of them are pretty weak in lots of ways. They are more prima donna-ish mind you, and I'm generalising here, but they're not a physical threat in the way Mains are. The Mains seem more normal. There's much more psychological damage on the VP's, given the nature of their crimes. The VP's are, on the whole, perfectionists and more fussy about their work, but the downside is they get hung up if things aren't good enough. Working on that is a good skill though, learning to settle for less sometimes and just getting things done. The VP's are also more fear-filled in general, and more sensitive to things, so that can work to your advantage because you can have more control in the classroom, whereas the Mains are much noisier, and much more likely to let you know if they're not happy about things. I probably came across more intelligence in the VP's, in that I got higher exam results with more of them. They were very different but I enjoyed teaching both.

Sarah

I've never had anything to do with sentence planning or education, I've always been on the wing. We have to make sure they go to education because the prison gets fined if the classes aren't full and the manager will be up asking questions. But half of them aren't bothered, they'd sooner stay in bed and watch Jeremy Kyle. A lot of men can't read or write, or they blag you and say they're not feeling well. If they don't go for two consecutive days they're put on basic regime, which is seven days bang-up and loss of canteen. They have to sign up for education or work when they arrive now, but there isn't enough of either so they go on a waiting list for three months. If they refuse from the start, they go straight on basic, but some would still rather do that than sit in a class or go to work. The prison tries quite hard to get them work but some of these lads have never worked in their life, they're not interested.

Gary

Jack phoned me up and said, dad, can you buy me a guitar? One of the lads was selling one for fifty quid. I said, yeah, I'll send a postal order. But I got a text from a contraband mobile, with an account number and sort code. I put the money in and the next time Jack called me he was playing his guitar. But he can't go to guitar lessons because he's not on rehabilitation from drugs, and they're the only ones allowed in that class.

Keith

Purposeful activity has got to be geared towards giving people skills for when they go back into the outside world. My first male prison, there were three huge workshops with men on sewing machines making prison shirts and trousers. We don't make clothes in this country anymore, so giving those skills is a complete waste of time. I fought a long battle with prison industries to get rid of those workshops. Education comes into that as well of course, and we should consider the arts more. In the women's prison we had prolific self-harmers, but when we got a writer-in-residence, some of these women found a new outlet through creative writing, so instead of cutting themselves they expressed their concerns through writing. And that had a massive positive effect. So purposeful activity should be viewed in a number of different ways, but unfortunately, with Chris Grayling and his predecessor, we began to view arts in prison as unimportant, it was all about work skills, literacy and maths. A prisoner up in Scotland came out and became a sculptor, Jimmy Boyle. A chap from Liverpool, Peter Cameron, he first picked up a paint brush in prison and now he's a successful artist. Then there's Erwin James the writer.

Billy

Education was alright in young offenders. It was hard though because the lads didn't want to learn, they just went down there for a bit of crack. And you have to go to education or work for money, so you're forced into it. But they put me on this computer course in adult prison and it was full of numbskulls and fucking nonces. And I'm pretty clued up on computers. I was sitting there doing easy stuff like changing font. I said to the teacher, I don't want to do this, it's shit. She said, I'll just send you back to the wing then. So I was put on twenty-two hour bang up for four or five weeks, because I didn't want to do a class that I didn't even put down for.

Adele

Workshops ran by prison staff get prisoners kicked out for anything, they get the cream of the crop, they pick and choose and have them for years. In education, you have to write three Information Reports, update the observation book, do the paperwork, take it down the wings and put them on report. I try not to do that because I wouldn't have time for a drink, never mind lunch. And all they get is a couple of days loss of association and they're back on classes, or they just shift them from my class to IT and back again. Because the prison has targets, the college has targets, it's all about funding. You get a certain amount from them enrolling, the next lot for guided learning hours they spend with you, then the final bit if they pass. But the most funding comes from enrolment and time in class, so as long as they get them in they've done their job. And nine times out of ten the student hasn't chosen the class and doesn't want it, they're placed in it against their will. If they refuse to attend they're stripped of every privilege, they get no gym, and no money apart from the minimum fifty pence cell rate a day.

Nigel

Education is very important; it's the cornerstone of rehabilitation. I feel quite strongly about it and I did a master's degree dissertation on the perceptions of education there. The prisoner has to want it though. Until he's ready to engage, forcing him to attend is not the answer. My feelings are that we need to change it a lot. I would say increasing contact time to the levels that it's currently at has probably hindered learner progress. And it's very easy to say they should all be doing GCSEs and A' Levels, but this is more to do with funding models. Certainly, long term courses would be a better way forward than quick four week courses in a long term prison.

Billy

All the lads were talking about women, as young lads do, and this lesbian teaching assistant got offended when I told a joke. She said, right, you're going back to your cell. I refused to leave, because there was nothing homophobic in what I said. She called the screws in and they cleared the classroom and pulled all the tables out. You've got one last chance, they said. I said, sorry, I'm not going. One of them hit the bell and they steamed in and started twisting me up. They put the handcuffs on, took me down the block, put me up against the wall and handcuffed me. One said, wait until we leave before you move, otherwise we'll take you down again. So I flinched towards one of them for a laugh, and that was it. He kneed me straight in the side. Four of them slammed me on the floor. They nearly broke my arm. One of them gave me a couple of digs in the back of the head, one was booting into me, the horrible bully bastards.

Alice

Twelve years teaching in a high security prison and I've only once or twice felt in danger. I had to confront one man because he wasn't doing Open University in the class and he'd ignored earlier warnings. That was the only point that I felt I might be physically attacked. But the men in the classroom picked up on it, and I saw them tense in their seats and get primed to step in. It didn't happen thankfully. I had a personal alarm which I could have pressed at any point, but I never had to press it in twelve years. There's ten to twelve students in your class, never more than that. There's three classrooms on the Mains education block and just two officers in the corridor, so if someone wanted to physically attack me in the classroom, they could have done before an officer got there, of course. The VP education block has eight classrooms and four officers. And a lot of the time the officers are sitting, chatting away, absorbed in their own lives. But I would always let an officer know if I was worried about someone and ask them to keep an extra eye on me, and they did. And I have had people removed from my classroom if I thought someone was getting too aggressive, and the officers were always great in that.

Keith

Ian Dunbar's 'A Sense of Direction' hit the nail on the head with dynamic security, treating people as individuals rather than a mass, and having plenty of activities rather than sitting in cells all day. But we've reduced that level of activity because of financial issues. What they call the core day has been pared down to an absolute minimum. And there's always been a belief among governors looking at purposeful activity figures in other prisons, that there must be some lying going on. With all the interruptions of visits, healthcare etc., some of the figures in the national statistics can't possibly be real. Someone's bending reality.

Adele

If I'm allowed fifteen in the class I'm running, the prison overcalls by five. If twenty turn up I have to give five of them a slip. A slip is an authorised absence so they can go back to their pad and still get paid.

Why do they call twenty up if they know the class can only have fifteen?

Because if somebody refuses, or can't come because of healthcare, sentence planning or whatever, they'll still fill the class. Some people actually want to be in class, are enrolled in it but can't get in. I wait until they're all in, and if we're over numbers I send the newest ones back, hopefully ones who haven't been enrolled yet. They still get paid for it, because it's an authorised absence. I send half a dozen back every week, it used to be more but some are refusing to come over. So yeah, the prison purposely over recruits, knowing not all can actually be in the class. Bums on seats. Class efficiency. That's what it's all about.

Paige

If you didn't do education you had to stay in your cell and you got your TV took off you, and you didn't get no money either, so you'd have no canteen. All I got was baccy because I didn't have no' one sending money in for me, I just relied on the prison system.

Alice

The prison authorities don't make use of education, not at all. It's a big failure, in terms of rehabilitation, and in terms of being far-sighted. We're sending these people back out. What about re-offending? Prison authorities don't liaise with education. They fail to see the great tool they have in their midst's. I do generally think it's abysmal. And the wages they get for education, it just highlights my point. Their wages go down if they want to study, so that tells you everything. Prisoners are workshy, that's their view, so we have to give them higher money as an incentive to get them into work, and while this may be true in some cases, it's not in the majority. Prisoners give up a lot to come to education. The prison's shooting itself in the foot, by failing to see how useful education really is.

Billy

I got six pounds a week for education. You get a lot more for work and that's what puts the lads off education. Loads don't get money sent in, so they want to work in the kitchens for fifteen pounds a week and you can't blame them, it's nearly three times as much. The reason they do that, is so prisoners want the work, then they don't have to pay people loads more to come in from the outside. Prisoners do the work for two quid a day. Kitchens was the best paid job. There was gardens, laundry, wing cleaners, servery, gym orderly, library orderly. Someone has to do all those jobs, so that's why they offer more money than education, because it's an incentive and they still save loads.

Adele

If they're in woodwork and put one foot wrong, the prison gets them out immediately. That's really wrong. And workshop prisoners get more money than education, they get more money sweeping the floor than doing Maths and English. And if they go to chapel, we can't compete with coffee and biscuits, they're only allowed water in class-rooms.

Why do they get more money for sweeping floors than for going to education?

Because the officers have to keep the wing clean, and they're doing a full-time job and get bonuses, and we're not allowed to give them that. If they're in full-time education and they're standard prisoners, they get £9.50 a week, and if they're enhanced they get £11.50. A wing cleaner can earn £18 a week, in the kitchens almost double that, because they're out from six in the morning until seven at night. They've said for years all prisoners will get the same money wherever they work or study, but it's never happened. Financially, education is bottom of the pecking order, apart from staying in your pad all day.

Sentence Planning

Peter

We look after the community a lot better than we look after the individual, but the individuals have a pretty good deal, lifers could do a lot worse. I'm proud to be part of the criminal justice system in this country. The independence of the judiciary is a fantastic thing, but people don't really get it. In my career, more than twenty five years, I've seen magistrates get it wrong a number of times. But in terms of crown court and big sentences, the last seven years for me, I've only known one where I've been convinced he didn't do it. I've never seen a criminal trial where I thought the result was for sale, not once. I'm not a naïve person, I don't pretend to have special insight, but I don't think it's for sale, and I don't think I could say that with confidence in a lot of other places. So that is sustaining and reassuring. It's got integrity.

Rebecca

The system, if it's a black child and a white child, is totally different. I have one brother, he was in trouble a lot, but it wasn't serious, it was car offences, driving without a licence, speeding, things like that. They found a firearm in the house where he was. He wasn't in possession of the firearm, it was just in a house where he was. But one neighbour said they saw him and my other brother fire it. My other brother had an alibi, but the first brother didn't so he went to court. The firearm wasn't found in his possession, it didn't have his fingerprints or DNA on it. There was another white guy who was found with an actual firearm, with ammunition, he got eighteen months and my brother got ten years. My brother's still inside, he's done over ten years and we don't know when he's coming out. He's got drug problems, so when he got home leave, obviously his first thing was drugs, and then he got to a place where he couldn't leave the drugs to go back from home leave, so he got recall, and he's still there now. That's why I say there's issues.

Gary

The criminal justice system let us down. The guy that was up after my son got a suspended sentence for breaking a woman's jaw. My son got eight years for less. But it was a different judge. Our judge was a recorder, a trainee judge. She wasn't listening to anything our solicitor was saying. At the end, the solicitor said, what about the criminal damage? She said, oh give him an extra six months. The maximum you can give is three.

Peter

Working closely with judges has led me to see them as a very liberal and compassionate group of individuals that I respect, far more easily than I would have expected. Taken as a group, there is no relish for handing out high sentences, Quite the contrary, there's an appropriate reluctance. And I'm glad I work in a system that doesn't have the death penalty.

Is there consistency to sentencing? Some people would argue women and ethnic minorities are sentenced harshly.

Yes, I would say there's a disparity, for women and especially for ethnic minorities. If you read case law on drugs for example, it would lead you to the conclusion that having the name Khan or Singh, and having that preceded by Regina v, is a precursor to a long bit.

Well it must be judges that are giving those sentences out.

Yes, it must be. *A long pause.* I'm aware I'm saying things without having figures to hand, and that these are emotive issues, but I would not be in the least surprised to have it demonstrated to me that people from ethnic minority backgrounds, particularly those from Afro-Caribbean backgrounds, are disadvantaged, particularly in terms of length of imprisonment and around specific offences. And you're right, it is judges that hand those sentences down. With women, I think it's subtler than that. I would say women tend to get a better deal, but within

that there's a minority, it's the extent of the deviance, the not conforming to the stereotype and expectation of femininity; women who
depart from those things tend to get a harsher sentence. Yes, that's the
case. But if you want to look at disadvantage and discrimination, at
society in general and the criminal justice system in particular, then
check out young white men with an IQ of under one hundred, because
they also really get a very fucking bad deal.

Daniel

Don't get me fucking started on Sentence Planning. I had this pre-
sentence report done, by this Probation Officer I'd never met in my
life, never even spoken to on the phone. I didn't know anything about
her and she didn't know anything about me. She turned up an hour
late for the visit, so we only had twenty minutes, and I was getting
sentenced two days later. She sat in this room, all smiles and questions, and I thought I answered them alright, although I was lying
about some things because I was getting sentenced. I said I was forced
into doing things, which everybody says anyway. Then, when I got the
report at court, it said I had a child, a lad, and it named the mother,
who I know. It said I had previous offences with being addicted to heroin, and I've never took heroin in my life, and I'm not being funny but
I'm eighteen fucking stone full of muscle. When I asked them about
it, they said, we've got information. From where? I asked. We gather
it from all sorts of places, they said. I started a judicial review against
this woman, and I don't even think she was a proper Probation Officer.
Then all of a sudden she resigned, so I get a new Probation Officer
and the next year I'm explaining this, and I've got in contact with the
woman who's supposed to be the mother of my child and told her. She
said, I'll go up and take his birth certificate, I'll even take his dad if you
like. So I said, she'll come up anytime you want, can you take that off
my pre-sentence report? They said, no we can't take anything out, but
we can write she's been to see us. So she's willing to go up, with her
son and husband and the birth certificate, she's even willing to do a
DNA test because she doesn't want her son to be on my pre-sentence

report, and they still won't take it out, because they can't admit they made a mistake. So my family get my pre-sentence report, see I've got a son and I've been on heroin and all this other shit I've never done, and I'm having to explain it's not true. And to say that to my dad, when he's a professional guy who's got faith in the system, it's like having to explain yourself every fucking visit. I said to Probation, instead of building family ties, you're pushing him further away, you're making him think I've been on heroin and he's a grandad and didn't even know. And then my new Probation Officer looked at it and said, yes it's wrong, it shouldn't have the heroin box ticked, it should be crack cocaine. And I said, what? I've gone from being a smack-head to a crack-head now? Honest, I've got all my pre-sentence reports, I saved them, and they're an absolute fucking joke. And apparently, when I was fifteen I was sniffing glue. Sniffing glue? Where's that come from? It's like they write things in there like News of the World, knowing it's not true and you can't do anything about it.

Donna

This man, a sex offender who nobody had done anything with, I said to him, I promise, I'll do what I can, I'll do a report saying this is the work, and I'll do it myself. He got out because he did all the work and because he believed in me and said I showed him respect. He was a human being with human rights and I was fighting for that, and then I addressed his behaviour, which of course I wasn't happy with, and it worked, because he had that motivation to do it. You can't be weak, because these lads aren't saints, but you still treat them the way you want to be treat. Imagine you're inside, you've got nobody, and then somebody says, don't worry, I'll sort it for you, and then nothing happens for ages. And then another Probation Officer turns up and says, I'll sort it for you, and they don't. No wonder they're cynical. And that happens a lot, broken promises, broken promises and lies. Loads I've worked with, you say, ah, I see you've done this work, and they say, I don't know what you're talking about. And you say, well, you've been somewhere and seen this person and tackled these issues, and they say, no, nobody's ever seen me about that. But if you read their assessment, oh my God, that worker's done so much. Because it's easier isn't it, to just put something down on a computer rather than actually do it?

Craig

I saw Probation once a year, at my sentence planning. There'd be the senior officer, his deputy, Probation and someone from education if you're really lucky. And even though you have sentence planning every year, they go through every single detail of your offence. You've maybe done God knows how much work over the years to address that, but it doesn't matter, they read everything out. They might move you up to enhanced, or down to basic, or onto a better wing, or they could say, we're gonna put you up for parole, but it's usually a tick-box exercise and right, we'll see you next year. Mind you, even though I spent a lot of time in prison, I never had one argument or fight, I never had one nicking, so maybe mine were a bit more monotonous. But that was twice as frustrating because I never moved any further forward. The government were on about changing Probation, having it ran by private firms, and all these Probation Officers were starting to get worried and I thought good, you should be worried, because while you've been doing it, you've not been doing anything, you're not trying to help people, you're just ticking boxes.

Stephen

Prisoners are very forgiving if they think you're there for the right reasons and you're doing your best. It's the way things are done that is important, and what troubles me from a psychological perspective, is that there's a bourgeois assumption that we know best, and if that's conveyed then the probabilities of it working are highly diminished. People get offended and insulted if they're told what they need to do with their lives.

Daniel

This is a sentence plan board. You sit there, a prison officer says, has he had any nickings in the last twelve months? If they say yes, he asks you about them. If not, they move onto objectives for the next twelve months. Anyone got any courses? Well there's a new one come out, it's called Abuse of Donkeys. Right then, we'll get him to do that, even though he's never seen a fucking donkey in his life. Because every twelve months some stupid new course comes out. You say, but I've done that course you'd wanted me to do, can I not get a C Cat now? And they say, no, this new course has just come out. So no, sentence planning doesn't help to plan anything. You sit there, listen to a load of bollocks for half an hour, realise you're not getting your fucking C Cat despite all the courses you've done and the fact you've never had a nicking, then you go back to your cell and wait another year. And that's the only time you see your Probation Officer. It's pointless. Sentence plans are pointless.

Adele

Education is in some of the lads sentence planning but the prison's way behind with them. There's a lad on recall, a really settled lad, and his parole hearing was five months ago but it's been put back again because he hasn't been on a course that our prison doesn't offer. He's been trying to get transferred to a prison that does that course for months. How frustrating is that? I can't think of anything worse, going way past your possible release date through no fault of your own, because you can't do the courses you've been told you have to do.

Peter

After pre-sentence report, I write a risk assessment. Most murderers are low risk of re-offending, they do it once and never again. Shoplifting, really quite high risk. Risk of harm to yourself, well we don't care about that anymore, I have to shoehorn that in because I think it's an issue. And then the conclusion states, bearing this and that in mind, this is what we're going to do with them. Again, I have a word count that limits the extent to which I can argue and lay out detail. Bear in mind this detail is somewhat of a contract, because in your first supervision session, post sentence, we can sit you down and go, this is what you agreed to, this is what you signed up for. So the more explicit that is the better. I'll agree to anything with a gun to my head. Why wouldn't I? I'm going to court and you're offering me a chance to stay out of jail or get out quicker? Hoops? How many do you want me to jump through?

And How Did That Make You Feel?

Donna

I went to this sentence planning and everybody's around the table, and another Probation Officer had this bloke before me because I'd been on the sick with my heart, so I was reading the notes and reports, thinking nothing seems right here, I think he should be in a psychiatric unit. I said to the lad, can I ask your name? He said something like Jesus, and I thought, aw fuck here we go. I said, do you know who the Prime Minister is? He said Andy Pandy or something stupid, he was totally off the wall. I looked at everybody and said, I'd like to stop this meeting now, and I said to the lad, it's lovely seeing you, and to the officer, can you take him outside? And then I said, what the fuck is going on here? He's off his face. What on earth is he still doing in this prison? They all said, aw he wasn't that bad when we saw him. The Probation Officer from the prison said, let's just have this meeting, then he can get moved to another prison. They just wanted shot of him. They couldn't be bothered to go through the process of putting him in a psychiatric unit, it was disgusting. I interviewed the lad afterwards and he didn't have a clue, he was away with it. I thought, maybe I've got it wrong, so I went back to work and read his file. The previous Probation Officer hadn't even seen him, he was going purely off what the prison service said. I went through every channel I could, and finally, after weeks and weeks of fighting with everybody, I got him into a psychiatric unit. Then unfortunately, I went back on the sick again with my heart complaint, and I heard he'd been put back in a mainstream prison. And because everybody was covering their backs and the work hadn't been done, he was nearly killed. This lad sent letters about Teletubbies. You'd be having your coffee reading them, thinking oh God, try and work this one out, and he was considered sane enough to be in a mainstream prison because some Probation Officer hadn't done his job properly. And honestly, there's loads of prisoners like that.

Keith

I was horrified when they closed down the big asylums, because they scooped up all the individuals that weren't dangerous but couldn't exist out in society, and these people started coming into prison. A number of recent research projects have identified something like seventy-five percent of the prison population having some sort of mental health issue, whether that's depression or something more serious. We've got NHS mental health teams working inside prisons now, and they've made a major impact, but the resources just aren't there to cope with the problem. And if somebody needs a secure hospital, they're in very short supply, so offenders with serious mental health needs are stuck in prisons waiting for beds in secure hospitals. Prison isn't the right place for some of these people. Perhaps we should consider reopening some asylums, because care in the community doesn't seem to be working either.

Stephen

The assumption is that some prisoners with mental health problems will be better off in hospitals. I've worked in both and that's not always true. Sometimes prisons are more therapeutic than hospitals. If someone has a range of mental health problems, whereby they don't have the skills to structure their lives, having the structure of a prison can be really quite helpful. I've spoken to prisoners who were homeless and freezing and committed crime so they can have food and a wash, because that's the state of our society in some places. Some of them have diagnosable mental health disorders, and are benefiting from services that provide them with a structure. That would be called community care in another setting, if those services were available. And if it were delivered by health and social care practitioners, people would see this as positive.

Antonio

Psychology? I was fixed term sentence, so unless you squeal like an onion you don't get no help. They're only interested in people who are kicking off anyway, it's a load of bollocks, tick-box, tick-box, tick-box bollocks. The public are no safer whatsoever, not by one fucking iota, by making prisoners sit in front of 28 year old trainee psychologists and fill in forms, it's utterly ridiculous. Those procedures make a laughing stock of the whole thing, they make prisoners sneer at their job. I was willing to do any course they wanted me to. I was a Category A prisoner, so I was a bit of a unique case, though not that unique. I reckon about three percent of high security prisons have a similar category and crime. But I needed to downgrade my categorisation to be able to get closer to home, to have access to jobs outside, to start rehabilitating and reconnecting with the community, to have visits from family. They said, you can't be downgraded until you take a course related programme. Okay, so far, so logical. What course do you want me to take? I'll take any course you're offering. Well, there's no courses here for you to take, you have to go to the lower system, Category B, because that's the only place they do them. Okay then, send me there. We can't because you're a Category A prisoner. I kid you not, it cost them a hundred fucking thousand pound a year to keep me in a Category A jail, or it cost joe public that because they're the ones who are paying.

Alice

I never had any connection with the psychology department, and there should be liaison there. As a teacher, you feel you have so much you can tell psychology, and help them with. But the men complain constantly about psychology, in that it's just a tick-box interview they do, that they're concerned primarily with figures and scores. And while it's probably not completely true, or the men's views may be exaggerated a little, I would say there's a lot of truth in that. Interviews with psychologists are not open ended, they're not geared towards truth and dignity. The men feel they have to hold back from telling the truth;

they talked about it in class quite a lot. And when you have a system like that, it has serious implications for a lot of the men, because it can mean years added onto a sentence if they're labelled as such and such, and they're so wary of being labelled, that they'll tone things down, or be afraid to admit certain things, that in some cases as a teacher, I'd see as a positive happening.

John

I never talk about the dark side of prison. I've got a photograph on my phone of the aftermath of a slashing, purely because the security officer took it for the records and e-mailed me it. I've still got it on my phone, me pointing at a bed covered in blood, but I've never shown anybody. I've got one of me in full uniform with all my medals on, which everybody's seen. There's a lot of dark things go on inside prison, a lot of dark things, but why share them? I'd rather talk about the fist fight in the corridor than the lad who's dark blue and hanging. There should be an outlet for that, but there isn't, and we can see that on a nightly basis and we've got nobody to talk to about it. There's no staff psychology, there's a care and support team but they're only in there to get promotion and be known. There's no counselling either. You can organise your own, or if you go off sick, they'll arrange it for you, so you can get back to work quicker. It's not for you, it's for them. So yeah, I never talk about the dark stuff.

Val

I didn't know at the time but I was ill. They took me to a psychologist and she can't have been much into her profession, because she told me to hit her. I said, I can't, I'll fucking kill you. She kept asking me to hit her, she said it would get my aggression out. I said, please don't say that to me, honest, I will fucking kill you. I walked out and said she wasn't capable and never saw her again. I saw a psychiatrist as well but I nearly punched him in the nose because he had his head in a book when he was talking to me. I said, you can either look me in the eye or you can fuck off, and then I walked out. How ignorant is that? If I was talking to somebody I wouldn't be bending my head in a book.

Paige

My problems started when I saw my mam getting bashed up by my step-father. And then I got raped and my mam didn't believe me. But I never saw a psychologist or someone from mental health in prison, it wasn't even mentioned. The only treatment I got in there was the dentist.

Billy

I only saw a psychologist once, for a pre-sentence report on re-mand. I didn't really speak to them, I was a closed book then. He was going on about Borderline Personality Disorder. Probation came and seen me for a pre-sentence report as well. The woman who done it was lovely. She was an older woman. That was the only time I saw her in prison though.

Stephen

This stuff about mental disorder in prisoners is overegged, tre-mendously. It's not backed by good evidence. Of course there's lots of people in prisons with mental health problems, but DSM4, the diagnosis statistical manual, has grown with each reissue. There's all these different types of conduct disorders now, it's a big psychiatric industry and there's no clinical basis for them, just a set of agreed criteria. If we start to pathologise everyday behaviour then we'll find lots of pathology. Let's suppose you were put in prison and someone said, how are you feeling? You might say you were pretty down; well that's part of the criteria for depression. Do you think people are watching you? They are in prisons, we know that. Well perhaps you're paranoid.

There's too much priority put on the pathology of an individual. The environment is more pathological than the person, on the whole. And if you're depressed in prison, or angry, then I think that's probably because you're a bit normal.

Donna

The only time you get anybody into a psychiatric unit is when they're top end, and then it's secure, or you might get them into hospital but they'll only be there a few weeks. Often, the problem is determining whether it's mental health or drugs. You fight like hell and say, well it's a cycle, isn't it? It's neither one nor the other. I'd have been off my head on drink and drugs if I'd had the life some of them had. They're being punished for having mental health problems, they're being punished for having addictions, and they're not getting appropriate help for either. You can't just section off one part of a person; alcohol, drugs, poverty, mental health. It's all a package isn't it? And you can't get the money. Funding comes from different areas, so I have a lad I'm trying to interview and he's on another planet, and all I'm doing is giving him vitamins thinking please don't die before the next time I see you.

Stephen

Suicide rates are higher in psychiatric hospitals than prisons. Yes, the countervailing argument might be that hospitals take particularly acute cases that would be equated with a high risk of suicide, and there's something to that, but it's not a given that if you put someone from this environment into that environment, then things will be better. What we do know, is that it will cost maybe five or ten times more. And when thinking about cost, you need to think about benefit. And so we need to think, is there a third way, where we can do things differently, and I think there can be.

Daniel

It's the things they ask you. This psychologist asked the group, what's your favourite animal? Some bloke said, my favourite animal is a Pitbull. She said, ooh your favourite animal is a dog, so you would like to have a best friend and be obedient for people, but you need somebody to tell you what to do. Somebody else said, I'd like to be a lion, and she said, you want to be a cat, you want people to work for your affection. She got to me and I said, I want to be a dolphin. She said, oh that's a new one, why do you want to be a dolphin? I said, so I can swim in the sea all day and everybody will love me. She didn't know what to say, she put down that I was taking the piss. And one guy, honest he was mentally disturbed and shouldn't have been in our class, he said, I want to be a hobnob. And she said, a what? And he said, I want to be a hobnob. She said, we're talking about animals Brian, not biscuits. And he said, I don't like animals, I want to be a hobnob. So she went, alright then, you can be a hobnob. And that was it. He sat in that classroom telling everyone he wanted to be a hobnob, he's obviously got problems, he's never getting out of fucking jail because he's a multiple murderer. And he's doing Thinking Skills Programme with about forty fucking years left? It's unproductive and stupid. What's he even doing there? He should be in Broadmoor.

Stephen

Everything is resource intensive and done for political dressing in the high security estate. I'm not saying don't work with high security prisoners, I'm saying work with them on an individual level. In hostage negotiation training, we start by calming, we build rapport and then we persuade. The problem in high security is that we don't invest in building rapport, we invest in is trying to persuade. We come back to care and control; if you and I have a positive rapport, it would be much easier for you to persuade me of something. High security estates go straight for the persuasion element, often with individuals who are angry, for all sorts of reasons, and people can attribute legitimacy or otherwise to it, but if the person's angry, they're angry. Someone might say, they've got no right to feel angry, what about their victim? That's a different moral argument. If someone's angry, that's where they are, and as a psychologist I've always tried to focus on where someone is at, because that's the core issue in terms of forming what I might most helpfully do.

Keith

Many prisoners are suspicious of psychologists because they have great influence on things like parole reports. I've come across numerous individuals who feel psychologists are trying to get inside their head and do something, yet my experience of psychologists is that they're fantastic, as are some of these cognitive behavioural programmes we do, particularly around sex offending. If you combine Sex Offender Treatment Programme with a mentoring scheme, it does seem to work very well.

Peter

I don't want to say too much about psychology. They tend to be recently qualified, take themselves dreadfully seriously and punch far above their weight, and they have huge influence in assessing risk, on sentence planning and categorisation. *A long pause.* Defensive and inexperienced practitioners are risk averse, and disposed to keep people in rather than move them towards getting out. That might be the task they're told is required of them, but I don't think that's therapeutic. I had a guy down south, a lifer who'd disengaged from the system. I attended the sentence planning board, he didn't. He had a young woman psychologist, recently qualified, who he'd refused to see. She said, I've had a look at his file and it just screams psychopath. I said, you know, there really aren't that many of them. You should actually meet them before you stick that label on.

Alice

Psychology have far too much power. They should have some power, and what they say should matter, but from my experience of twelve years inside a high security prison, what they say is almost always geared to work negatively, and it's done by labelling, by a short sighted and limited mode of taking in how a prisoner is behaving. They're not getting a complete picture, in fact they're often getting a false picture, and the men are very aware of this and they're working things all the time, to their advantage. And when I say this, I mean in terms of not wanting their sentences to be longer, or them to be penalised in any way, when actually, they weren't doing anything wrong. And also, some of the things could be viewed as positive moves. Honest. Psychology? Such a waste of money and funds. Psychology's main success is ensuring those with the worst personality problems, that are a threat to society, are kept inside and given some kind of treatment, so that's protecting the public. But in the majority of cases, psychology fails.

Stephen

You don't need to train psychologists for three years, you could do it in two, like it was done for years. There's no evidence we've done better by extending it. But it funds universities for another year and people get to call themselves doctor and there's a high value placed on that.

Daniel

I had an interview with this psychologist. She was an absolute tit, about nineteen years old, fresh out of university. I had to see her for a one-to-one to complete my Thinking Skills Programme. In the end I told her to get a job in McDonalds because she didn't know what she were talking about. She asked me, how did that course make you feel? What do you mean, how did it make me feel? It made me feel like a twat, because you were asking me what animal I wanted to be, and I was sat next to someone who wanted to be a hobnob. And how did that make you feel? You might as well get a tape recorder, and every ten minutes get it to say, and how did that make you feel? Because that's all they say. What did you have for dinner? Peas. And how did that make you feel?

Donna

I don't know whether the majority of psychologists are newly qualified, or trainees, but most people they see seem to have personality disorders, no matter what's going on. And it's very similar on the outside, when you get a psychologists report. I think the good ones are few and far between, I'm not impressed at all to be honest. They have all this jargon, and you think, God I can hardly follow what you're saying and I've got a degree and a professional qualification, so what the hell do the lads think? And the lads say, I've got a diagnosis, I've got a title, and I say, stop it, you're faking it, life's more complicated than that. Yes, if you can get a diagnosis of Asperger's and get more help, but not general sweeping statements. Most psychologists have nothing invested in prisons because they're only there for a couple of years, they make assessments and leave. But that person can be left with that assessment forever. I don't think they realise the importance of it.

Stephen

There's a whole language that is ludicrous, about criminogenic factors, that gives legitimacy to the narrative we're being scientific about all this. People talk about faulty cognitions and self-harm. These are circular arguments that don't make sense. People are cutting themselves because they want to survive at the very basic level; it's a function of distress, not deficit. People are talked of as 'threatening suicide.' It's not a threat. You'd never say someone was threatening depression. Saying self-harm is attention-seeking or deliberate; it's an abusive language and it doesn't help to frame problems in that way if we want to work with people and help them.

Keith

It's accurate, the allegation that psychologists are generally young, female, middle class trainees from a totally different background to most prisoners. That's what they are. The prison service pays for psychologists to get their chartership, we put them through the training. In many cases, once they've completed the training, they shoot off and work for some company that will pay them a lot more, like in industrial psychology. So it's difficult to hang onto the good psychologists because we don't pay them enough.

Stephen

Over eighty percent of psychology graduates are female, and universities still recruit on social class more than ability. One of the most striking things, when I first went into prisons and so wasn't institutionalised, was how affluent we were as a staff team compared to the prisoners. Some prisoners had string tying up their trousers and underpants issued that were stained by previous use. The poverty of it was very stark. And in comparison to universities recruiting from affluent backgrounds, prisons are much better at recruiting inmates from lower socio-economic groups. There's a class distance between professionals and prisoners. Universities are part of the problem, and part of the solution. And society needs to be better at getting people into prison that have committed offences but are from a higher socio-economic position and are better protected. People should be called to book independent of their social class.

Paige

My friend used to self-harm. She had scars down her neck and all over her body. She was on Subutex and she offered me them but I wouldn't take them, because my mam died of an overdose. They used to take her away for three days, then she'd come back all bandaged up and with a staff member who'd stay with her for days.

Adele

This young girl, she killed herself on December 10th. I can't stop thinking about her on that date. I'd been working with her for six months before she told me her story. Her dad and brothers basically shared her, from a very young age. Her only place of safety was with her aunty and uncle in a different town. She was in for arson, and a lot of the girls who suffered terrible abuse seemed to commit arson. As she got older, her dad drove her around and gave her to others. And my God, there wasn't anywhere on her body she hadn't self-harmed. She wrote to her aunty and uncle and her work was meticulous, if it wasn't good enough she'd tear it up and start again, everything had to be perfect. Her uncle died first, and she used to tell me, I just want to die Adele, but other people would say, ah that's just Tracey, you know what she's like. And then a couple of years later her aunty died and I knew. I said to staff, she's going to do something, her aunty's died. And they said, she's been saying that for years. Then sure enough, she hung herself.

Billy

Lots of people hung themselves in adult prison. Four people killed themselves in five or six weeks. People were crowded round this guy's pad so I went over and he was hanging from the light fitting with his wrists slashed. He was on remand, waiting trial for rape and he'd already been done for rape before. Loads of screws rushed in and we got banged up, and exercise was delayed so everyone was kicking off about that, not the fact someone was hanging there dead. And when we did get out, everyone was just laughing about it, because they found out he was a rapist. People put on a front, a cold heart, like they don't care about stuff. I didn't sleep for two nights.

Alice

I was working with this notorious man who'd killed a large number of people, and he was doing a foundation year for a college in London, and I had essays from that man on the themes, set by the college, of love and death. I remember one particular essay, him writing about his childhood, and I saw this really sensitive young boy, who obviously cared about his father's feelings and was out to protect his father. And I wondered, how could he have gone from that to this? And also, why is Psychology not in here, analyzing these essays? Why are they not digging deeper, even from an academic point of view, to further their own discipline? My God, there was an utter lack of interest from around the prison.

Val

My mother was a prostitute. I got raped when I was seven and I developed a split personality. They said it was to cope with the trauma. See this is Val, but you also get Eve, and she goes, fuck you, I'll fucking kill you, and she won't take shit from anyone. She turns up when the circumstances are beyond control, and if somebody hurts me, she tells me, I fucking told you they'd do that. I tried to deal with it, but they said it was too deep, I was like Pandora's Box. Val will let you in but Eve will come and block you, because she knows they're going to try and get rid of her. And she's served a purpose, she protects me, I would have died without her. She talks to me. She says, go over there and tell her this and tell her that. I say, I don't want to, but she says, fucking do it now. And she was there all the time with me in jail.

Donna

Women are doubly punished. They're punished for their crime and punished for crime against society, because women aren't allowed to be violent. And you're a mother? And you left your kids because you got banged up? Most of them are mental. Most of them are off their heads on prescribed drugs. They probably had domestic violence, no family support, and then lots of them end up in lesbian relationships, because for the first time ever somebody gives a toss. And then they have to go back out to the madness.

The Presumption Of The Scale

Daniel

I've done every course known to man, in private and HMP. Thinking Skills, Self-Change, Drugs and Alcohol Abuse. I've never taken drugs or had a problem with alcohol but they made me do it anyway. I've done Relationships courses, even though I've never had a problem with relationships. All people do is answer the questions the way Probation or Psychology want them answering, and I'll tell you why. When I did my first course I thought right, I'll do this properly. I'd got to a point where I wanted to change my life, and I thought, for the first time ever, I'm going to have faith in the system. So I went into that four week course at a high security prison and I answered every single question as honestly as I could, to see what I needed to change. And do you know what happened? All my risk scores went up. I asked, why have my scores gone from medium risk to high risk? They said, it's the way you answered the questions. They asked me what it was like when I got a new girlfriend. I said, it's like having a new motorbike, you get on it for a bit, ride around on it and then you want to swap it for another one. And that warrants me going from medium risk to high risk? I've never had offences against women in my life. So I learned from my mistakes and I was never honest again. The courses are full of shit, all they do is give Probation and Psychology jobs. How can you sit there, with some clown you don't know, who's never committed an offence in their life, trying to tell you how to change? When they've never been on the fucking streets, they've never been in children's homes.

Peter

I've devised, delivered and evaluated programmes around car crime, anger management, drugs and alcohol, domestic violence and healthy relationships. PASRO, Prison's Addressing Substance Related Offending, that came and went and for some people it was quite effective but for most it wasn't. We blew that, as we blew a number of opportunities. When the Drug Treatment and Testing Order ̖ troduced, Probation controlled the budget, then gave it up afte months. We went from calling the shots and commissioning, ͺͺ ͺ told by bloated and self-satisfied statutory and independent organisations what they were going to give us for their money. Enhanced Thinking Skills was a good course. We nailed our colours to a cognitive behavioural mast and yes, made assumptions that a lot of people have thinking deficits, when actually, many of them were making informed pragmatic choices in difficult situations. Nevertheless, it's a good course with some good results. It's not a great shock that lots of guys in jail tell lies because they think it makes them more likely to get out, and that whole brownie point thing about being seen to be internalising stuff absolutely goes on. But that said, there are other positive effects, despite that, and to some extent because of it, because if people are thinking, perhaps for the first time, if I show I'm thinking this way, or seeing that point of view, they may actually begin to do that and acknowledge there are consequences to their actions.

Keith

There's vast differences between men and women's prisons. Men are more suspicious of staff and less likely to seek help. It fascinates me how the women seek out help and talk to staff and want to get involved in things. They have no qualms about talking to anybody. There was this big dining hall where I'd sit there with visitors and the women would always want to know who they were and would talk to them. David Ramsbotham, the Chief Inspector, thought it was great. That six years I spent governing the women's prison were the most enjoyable of my career. You could see women changing, wanting to make a difference to their lives. Men are a lot more cynical and I'm not sure why.

Stephen

There's a danger that psychologists are seen as functioning for the state, certainly in high security prisons. It's a lot harder to get trust, focusing purely on public protection, especially if someone feels every-ing they say is recorded. Weighing the state needs too highly disenfranchises the prisoner and affects the quality and sometimes accuracy of what's done. Go in the other direction and put the person first, and then prospective victims could be at risk. A good psychologist weighs both things.

Caroline

Group-work within probation is a bloody nightmare. A good friend of mine ran Sex Offender Treatment Programmes for six years and says it doesn't make much difference with most of them, they just play the game and go through the motions. He said there wasn't many that felt sincere about the things they were saying. And it must be difficult for sex offenders because even within sex offending, there's a pecking order. Some won't go as far as others and think other offences are totally inappropriate. But they put a lot of diverse people together and expect them all to be open and honest. And when I delivered Thinking Skills and Car Theft courses, a lot of offenders just took the piss. The courses had to be pitched so everybody understood, but they couldn't have pitched it any lower if they tried, it was almost like offenders decided, Probation thinks we're thick, so we'll act that way. And if you're setting up a group-work programme in a community team or a prison, then all the offenders know each other, or they've heard of each other, so they're rocking up to this group-work programme, having a laugh and running circles around staff. You get the odd one who wants to do it properly but they're few and far between. It would be much more effective on a one-to-one basis, where you can pitch it at the right level for who you're working with. And you always get one or two who fade into the background in group-work because they haven't got the confidence, but a one-to-one doesn't allow anyone to fade away, they all have to think and come up with things.

Peter

We like one-to-one, it's our default, it's what we joined to do in most cases. In the community, we're nearly all out of it, and there was resistance to group-work, with the main argument being that old thing about relationship and rapport, but research says that isn't actually a major factor. A twenty year follow up, a good longitudinal study, shows people remembered their early Probation Officers with fondness, but they'd gone on offending. And so whether they like you or not is not important. It's probably a bit better if they're favourably disposed, but not colluding, not being too friendly is important. Let's not be precious about this, they don't absorb our values by osmosis, or because they're pleased to see us.

But are people more likely to be honest in a one-to-one setting, rather than group-work?

Both yes and no. Yes, in a relationship of respect, if I call you out on your bullshit, particularly if I do that gently and you don't feel soiled in the process. But one of the rationales for group-work is that people are more likely to tell the truth when they're being challenged by their peers.

Donna

I despair. Prisons are being privatised, there's huge waiting lists for courses, and if they haven't done a course, they're not allowed to progress because it's part of their sentence plan. And those public protection sentences, I had one lad in a Young Offenders Institution, a scally with a bloody temper on him. I worked with his mum because social services weren't doing anything there. But he gets into fights inside and he's never going to get out. He got a two and a half year sentence and he's served eight. He waits ages for a course, then gets into bother just before it's ready so they won't have him. Now his behaviour doesn't help, but the situation all around him is actually increasing his risk.

Peter

There's a trend away from clinical judgement, from treating people as individuals, towards Offender Group Reconviction, statistical probability and such things, and they have their place, but when they were introduced, your own clinical judgement was still valued. Bit by bit that scale has swung, so for the last five years or more, it's the presumption of the scale; don't refer people for group-work on the basis you think they'd benefit from it, refer them for group-work on the basis of what they score on this or that scale. Similarly, with sex offenders; what does RM2000 say they are? And RM2000 is a good tool, it's probably the best risk assessment tool we've got, but it's just a tool. This internationally renowned psychiatrist gave a seminar on risk assessment some years ago. He said the best tool we've got is about fifty percent accurate, we know half of them are going to re-offend, we just don't know which half. I think we're a bit better than that, but not a lot. The watch-word, quite rightly in some ways, has been defensible decision. Why did you do this? Why did you not do that? And so, if I record I've not referred this man to such and such, because he only scores this, that's a defensible decision.

Stephen

There are problems with the way psychologists work is structured inside prisons, being very focused on specific types of risk assessment and so called offending behaviour programmes. Critics would say psychologists are technocrats, implementing policy. That's a little unfair, but there's something to it, a dumbing down overly-structured approach with no room for creativity or flexibility. Professional psychologists have to take their judgements to a situation, and that's been stripped out.

Colin

I did an intensive six month one-to-one course. That was the only course available to me. I got transferred to a Cat A unit in a different prison, then transferred back again once I'd finished. It was intensive and enormously difficult and it's meant to be, but I decided to get as much as I could, to engage with it. I should have been at home with my family and my kids. There was a need within me to make sense of things. I've never considered myself the dangerous person I was made out to be.

Do you understand why society considered you dangerous?

I suppose I have to answer yes. If someone is thought by society as a terrorist, then you're going to treat that person in a certain way, for the protection of society. I've never seen myself that way, I disagree with my branding. I've sometimes had views at odds with those that run society, but I wouldn't have said I was in any shape or form a dangerous terrorist.

Society's definition of a terrorist is anyone planning or likely to use violence to achieve political ends.

Yes, I suppose you're right. But at court it was recognised I wasn't planning anything. It's always been about my capabilities, and a lot of people have capability but you shouldn't necessarily send them to prison for it. Anyway, I chose to engage with the course and part of it was writing my life story, and I've been through some very difficult periods. It made me feel suicidal at points, exploring my childhood and picking old scars open.

Looking back, now you're further away from doing that; do you think it might have helped?

As a personal growth thing, possibly. With offending, I don't think it had a bearing one way or the other. You make the decision yourself, whether to offend again, and a course won't make any difference. Maybe it challenges you to think about things, but it doesn't move behaviour, you do that yourself.

But you're quite unique in that you had intensive one-to-one work, whereas Probation Officers I've spoken to have complained they don't have time for one-to-one work anymore.

They wouldn't have me in a group I guess, because of the nature of my offending.

Peter

It's always the singer, not the song. Many singers have made a mess of many great songs. A great song's a starting point, but you need a great singer, just as you need a great group-work leader. Programme integrity isn't an end in itself, it's just a milestone on the way.

Craig

They say doing these offending courses help you get out, help you with Probation and bail but they don't, I done every course going and I never got out any earlier. In fact, when I did get out they said there was still work to do, so courses are only good if you go into them to get out what you can. And I did that, because I knew I had problems that needed addressing. Even now, I've just finished that three month Better Life programme. I done well, I learned everything is how I look at things, how I react to things, whereas before, for depression, I'd go out and have a pint. But that would make us more depressed so I'd keep drinking, or I'd go to karaokes and be the life and soul of the party. And it was all a front. I'd get into one night stands, all the rest of it, I'd be kidding meself I was feeling better, oh it's a great life this, I'm loving it. And me friends would think, he's alright, he's always getting laid. But the reality was, I would go to the pub, head down, take a deep breath, make a sign of the cross, shoulders back and try and look big. Now then matey, how's it going? Shake hands, pats on the shoulder, work me way through to the bar. I'd have a couple of pints, talk to whoever was there or get up and sing. But if somebody said, come and sit with us, I'd be stumped, I wouldn't know what to do, what to say. The only way I knew how to act was to chat up lasses. So if I did sit with somebody, even though I didn't want the lass, I needed her to acknowledge she fancied us, just to make us feel better. And it was putting the males against us because they could see I was chatting their lasses up. I didn't know if I was gonna get battered, it was by the skin of me teeth every time.

Peter

The assessment of sex offenders is a skilled programme which requires training, qualification, supervision and experience. We had a dodgy start but I think we're pretty good at working with them now, I really do. We have got that slightly Kafka-esque approach where we encourage people to be honest, and we can't really do that much with them if they're not. Then at the end we ask if they're a risk of re-offending, and if they say medium risk, we say, well you may be underestimating this but at least you're acknowledging, and if they say high risk, we say, well he thinks he's high risk so he probably is, and if he says low risk, we say, well he's in denial so he's clearly high risk. And yes, you do get a lot of sex offenders in denial, but the research tells us, in terms of predicting recidivism, that denial is not a factor, although I know that's counter intuitive.

Donna

I did group-work but mainly one-to-one, lots of it, working with men and women who'd committed sexual offences. I'd meet them inside a few times, work on sentence planning and then complete the work once they were released. Years back, if you had a specific piece of work you wanted to do and that work wasn't available inside, you'd go in and do it yourself, but that all stopped. They do the Sex Offender Treatment Programme inside now, but that's group-work and some aren't honest in front of others, and you can get a lot more done with one-to-one at a crucial time. There might be a point where you've worked with somebody, you've got something out and if you just do that piece of work, that could really move things on. But then the one-to-one work finished, and it became all about monitoring.

Peter

This young man, he had a girlfriend with a little sister, and he'd groomed the little sister and sexually abused her. He served his sentence and began sex offender treatment, but then he disengaged from it because he'd got a job. He came to me three years later and it's internet offences, fairly extreme images being viewed. I did a sexual recidivist assessment on him, and he came out very high. Now high is a minority, but very high is very unusual, and not wanting to stereotype but he was a very manipulative young man, very ego-centric and self-centred, who wept at points during the assessment. He said, if I go to jail, a string of consequences will happen. I said, yeah, I believe you, in terms of your life outside and the repertoire of things that will be available to you, but what on earth were you thinking? You haven't got the I didn't know rationale. You disengaged from offence focused work. He got an extended sentence and that was right. So we don't get it right all the time, and we can't get it right all the time, but let's not hold exceptions up as the norm, because most of the time we call it right, and when we don't, we deal with it appropriately. He's doing an extended sentence, he'll be supervised for an extended period on licence, and he's right, his repertoire of life opportunities have greatly diminished, I doubt he'll get anywhere near under 16's professionally.

Craig

Now I've done these courses, I can see females as being friends, as associates or someone to pass the time of day with. Just because they smile it doesn't mean they fancy us, they're just being friendly. I think about how me behaviour appears to others. If I seen a bonny lass I would stare at her, I'd ogle her and think, oh she's gorgeous. But I wouldn't realise how it would look to them. They'd be seeing this fifty year old bloke, or forty-odd back then. Yes I'll be thinking they're nice, but surely they'll be thinking he's freaking me out. But I didn't see any of that, I just seen the result I wanted to see. Now, I look forward to going in pubs because I have friends to sit with and appropriate things to talk about. I don't sit with lads who talk about what lass they're gonna shag and stuff like that, I don't get no pleasure from all that and it could be a trigger for going back to me old ways. So coursework's worked a lot for us. The other day, these college lasses were getting on the bus. The old me would have got on and had a good eyeful, but I didn't, I waited and got another bus, I made a conscious decision. And I was talking to this lass behind the bar who said she hates it when lads give them money but make sure they're touching their hand, so now I put money on the bar and say, just put the change there darling. I look on everything different now, from the other person's side.

Peter

In terms of my confidence in proposing an intervention to the court, I would have more confidence in Community Domestic Violence Programme and Sex Offender Treatment Programme (SOTP) in the community than I would any other course. I've a lot of respect for people who work with those distressing issues. I've been on training courses ran by David Briggs, a consultant psychologist at Rampton, a well-published and empowering trainer around sex offenders. He held up a rubbish bin and said, you've as much chance of getting people to find this sexually arousing, as you have of realigning peoples sexuality. The issue is control. What we know of SOTP, is that in terms of contact offences, we reduce re-offending, we do. It's a very well researched area of our work. In terms of internet and non-contact re-offending, we don't seem to have much impact. Guys will say, I recognise this isn't a victimless crime anymore, and that's how I used to rationalise it, I know these are images of child abuse. And then they disappear and furiously masturbate in front of a computer.

Swamp Donkeys

John

Prison staff make or break prisons, and prisoners. Turn-keys. Screws. Warders. Guards. We're still called guards in the press. I haven't guarded anything since I was in the army. The union's breaking up, it won't last long, it will be an awful place to work in two or three years. Divorce rates are high, affairs are massive, everyone's shagging everyone else in the prison service. You're spending forty-eight, fifty hours a week with them, I was seeing prison staff more than I was seeing my wife. There used to be a hotel near the prison, about fourteen quid a night, and it was just prison staff constantly banging each other. A mate of mine who's left, he's got three ex-wives in there, all with his surname, he's divorced all three of them. You hear stories of female prison officers with young prisoners, it's inexcusable, prisoners with teachers and psychologists.

Val

There was a lot of sexual abuse going on in the prison. Inmates had orgies. People called it abuse because some got shipped out. They said this lass was pressured into it. Others said, no she agreed. It's difficult to draw the line sometimes. Some people fell in love, and a lot of lasses always had girlfriends. The biggest fucking dyke came up to me, she started singing love songs and asked me out. I said, no, I don't think so. She wore a size nine shoe and looked like a bloke. And there was sexual relations between screws and prisoners. This lass, she was stunning, she had long blonde hair, you could see with certain screws there was something going on, just by the way they looked at each other. I asked her, what are you in for? She was on the game and this punter started getting aggressive with her in the bathroom, so she wound the chain around his neck and slept downstairs for three days. There was a lot of sex going on between staff as well, but I don't care what anyone does as long as they leave me alone.

Adele

My eyes were out on stalks. There was lots of self-harming, lots of lesbian relationships, and I don't think many would have done it in normal circumstances, they were just desperate for comfort. And there were women they called swamp donkeys, long termers who preyed on first timers, who befriended them and took their money or meds, then persuaded them into a relationship. I was shocked. I couldn't believe you'd talk to someone and they'd seem so normal, then you'd hear what they'd done and how they'd wormed their way into other people. I used to think, what the hell am I doing here? I couldn't get my head round it.

Paige

No' one tried anything on with me. If they did, something would have happened to them. There was lesbians having sex, in full view of you, but I wasn't going to complain. Sex was common. If we were all in one pad, watching TV before lockdown, they'd come in with their hands down each other's pants, they're not bothered. And the screws are just sitting in their office all day.

Billy

A lad in young offenders had a relationship with a teaching assistant, and supposedly it continued after prison, she picked him up when he got out. That's what people said anyway. I wasn't aware of anything else, not in men's prisons. I don't think I met a gay person in there. I probably did, but they wouldn't come out and say they were gay. Maybe on the nonces wings, I could imagine there was some horrible stuff going on there.

Craig

They were four couples that I knew of, in the high-security prison, not the locals. One was a transsexual man about sixty who dressed as a woman, he was with a forty-something year old Asian who was prison gay but tried to deny that anything was actually happening. The other two couples were in their thirties and more open about it. The last couple started straight but turned to each other, and they denied it as well, but it was obvious they were prison gay. It didn't seem to bother most people though, and I'm not aware of any staff involvement, but that might have been because it was hidden rather than not happening.

Sarah

In all the time I've worked there, fifteen years, there's been three or four relationships between prison officers and prisoners. It's probably happened more but that's all I know of. You do get a lot of unwanted attention as a female though. Two prisoners said I'd been having an affair with them and bringing phones in for them. I was investigated. They said I went into their cells before I started work. It was all in their heads, they checked CCTV and realised. But the rumours were rife and it was hard to keep my head up at times. One officer got caught in a cell with her trousers around her ankles when she was on nights. She said she was trying his jeans on, but she was a slapper. I suppose it's human nature, it happens in other workplaces doesn't it?

Don't Look Back

Antonio

They came for me early doors. Layla was waiting outside, weren't you babe? In high security prisons you're on the same landing for years, some people for decades at a time, and it sounds insane but the landing I was on was a very quiet part of the jail, which was deliberate, and it took me years to get there. So when the screws came, and remember there's forty cells on my landing, I could tell what screw it was by his shoes and his shuffle and the jangle of his keys, and whether he was coming to my cell or who else's cell he was going to. But when they took me down to reception at eight o' clock in the morning and put me in a cell, there was shuffling feet and jangling all the time, I thought everyone was coming for me. So I was up and down constantly, and then it got past nine o clock, and ten o clock, and I thought the fuckers are gonna keep me, there's something going on. Some people get released and then arrested as soon as they set foot outside, it's called gate arrest, it's not common but it's not unheard of. And it's almost mythical to be released from that prison, there's only been one or two releases in the nine years I've been in there. So yeah, up to eleven o' clock it was fucking torture, but I couldn't let them see that. I laid down and got into this position, you learn it in prison, how to lie on a wooden bench and sleep, like a light switch going off. You can do it in just t-shirt and shorts, as long as you've a bit of warmth in your arms. It's from waiting rooms up and down the country, when you're on transfers and courts, going backwards and forwards. So eventually I went to sleep, or a kind of sleep, and then the screw came in and went fucking hell, come on, don't you want to go? And I felt it was deliberate as well, a little bit of a last fuck you, because we weren't friends, me and the screws. And they could have easily let me out of that gate at eight o' clock in the morning, they were there at fucking six, they told my Mrs to get there for eight, I'd been inside almost thirteen years. But I couldn't let myself get more agitated or I would have fucking exploded.

Paige

There was no' one waiting for me when I got out. The prison gave me some money and I got the bus straight to Probation and waited for the person to come and put my tag on. Then I had to go straight home because I had to be in the house from 7pm until 7am. I stuck to the tag. It's the only thing I have stuck to.

Daniel

I was told I was going to a hostel fifty miles from where I lived, because I'm not allowed back in the town where I committed my crimes while on licence. But when I moved to my last prison, I met an officer on the wing and she left the prison service to be with me, while I was a serving prisoner. We thought nobody knew, but they listened to my phone calls. Her partner worked on the wing opposite mine, and he was best friends with a woman who worked for Public Protection in the same prison. I used to do this course with kids who'd been expelled from school. I talked to them about changing their lives, about how I was changing my life, I showed them around the prison and did my best to stop them going down the same route. The teachers trusted me and offered me a job. I made a difference to a couple of kids and I felt really good about it. Then all of a sudden I got took off it. Basically, her ex-partner got with his best mate in Public Protection, and because I was on the prison phone, talking to my new partner and her daughter, they made a mountain out of a molehill. Her mum was saying, she's putting on weight, what's the best thing to do? I'm a qualified personal trainer and fitness instructor, I did it in jail. I said, put her on this diet and then once a week, give her a free day so she can have Kentucky Fried Chicken or whatever. And because I said that, and I'd started a relationship with a prison officer, they changed my risks, that were medium all the way through my prison sentence, to high to children, high to public, high to staff and high to adults. They were saying I'd coerced my partner into this relationship with me because I wanted to use her for bringing drugs in or something.

Antonio

And then it was all a bit of a haze. I signed multiple signatures, the governor came along and made sure it was me and not some other prisoner they were letting out, a few security questions and then they got some fucking numpty to escort me. This screw who took me to the gate, I know he takes a few quid and he's a fucking dick, he's worked his whole life for an apartment in Benidorm, he thinks he knows it all and he's speaking to me like I'm a teenage recidivist. Listen mate, you know when you get out, I don't want to see you back again, if you ever come back here. I said, you've been here twenty fucking years, I've had 180 men like you working for me, I'd have had you brushing floors mate, don't fucking speak to me like that. I just told him exactly what I felt. Up 'til then it's been a bluff, you keep a blag on your face, they know what you think but you can't tell them because they'll nick you. It's a game. And then they gave me forty quid and sent me on my way.

Layla smiles at Antonio. There was loads of workmen outside and they knew something was happening because all the screws had come out the visitors centre. And then I come running over the grass. It were dead romantic weren't it?

It was beautiful, and she was gorgeous, and she had this beautiful black hire car, all brand new. But she'd been on the phone, wondering why the fuck they weren't letting me go, and she'd done the car battery in. So I got in and said, let's get the fuck out of here, and the fucking car wouldn't start. She looked at me in horror and said, oh, what's the matter with it? It was working alright before. I said, you've been on the phone haven't you? She said, it's not that, it's not that. I said, baby, it fucking is. So I went to the visitors centre and got changed and she fluttered her eyelashes at a couple of screws, and they came out with a fucking Category A van and jump-started her. And then I came out all dressed up.

Like James Bond you were.

And you looked like Miss Moneypenny. And then off we sped into the distance.

Don't look back, you said, don't let me look back.

It's a prison myth. They say if you look back at a prison you're gonna return. So the first thing she did, which was beautiful and correct, she gave me a couple of joints to calm me down. They were only little ones, and she doesn't smoke so they weren't heavy joints, but fuck me, compared to prison joints. I can make a tiny bit of weed last a fucking week in prison. You just have tiny one-pops, the size of a match head, every few hours. But these ones blew my head off. So I'm on a date with my Mrs looking fantastic, not looking back, and the fucking colours were more awesome than that. *He points at the mountain.* Not necessarily today in this frame of mind, but at that time in that frame of mind, five, ten times more awesome.

Daniel

And then Probation had a field day. When I got out of prison, all of a sudden I wasn't going to the town they said I was, because that's where my girlfriend lived, I was going twenty miles away. I had to sign on at twelve and four every day, and be back in the hostel by seven. I got in my car every morning, left at eight, went to my girlfriend's house when the kid wasn't there, because they said I wasn't allowed there when she was, and that only got lifted eight weeks ago, after more than a year, despite the fact I've no offences against children or women. They got social services involved, they went to the school and had meetings with the teachers. I don't know how my Mrs did it, they made her life a fucking misery. And because I stuck to it and went to every signing on time, after two weeks they said, we need to move you because someone's coming out of prison you've got problems with. I said, I'm a high risk offender now, and I'm complying with everything. Why don't you move them somewhere else? But they refused and moved me forty-odd miles from my girlfriend, to another hostel. So I left at eight, drove to see my Mrs, now an hour and a half away, stayed there one hour, drove back to sign on, drove back again, had another half an hour, drove back to sign on at four, then drove to the hostel for seven. That went on for two months, and I was there on the dot, every time, I didn't give them one excuse to recall me. I said to my Probation Officer, why did you send me all that way? And because she was retiring she told me. We did it to inconvenience you, she said. The order came from above. I said, that's not right, you could have pushed me back the wrong fucking way, like I was before. She admitted people above her weren't happy I'd begun a relationship with a prison officer who'd left. But the relationship is genuine and always was, we're living together. They were trying to get me back in jail, one hundred percent. They wanted me to fail one of my signings or be late on curfew, but it never once happened.

Peter

Most Probation Officers with any experience would say something similar to this: consistently, the guys you've done the most for, will turn around and say, you've done nothing for me. But the service I joined, we were criminal justice social workers, that's what we were set up to be, and those values, they are way gone, it's just not part of the culture anymore. We're the service we're required to be, and we're the service we're permitted to be. We are not permitted to visit people in jail anymore. I couldn't even go to the nearest local jail. When I started I could visit a guy at the other end of the country. I'd just put a day in my diary and present the mileage claim when I came back. If I was going to be away overnight I'd discuss it. Now, I can't even leave my desk. Increasingly, we do interviews for reports by video link. They're putting forty video-link suites into the nearest local prison as we speak. The notion of welfare as a dimension of supervision was presumed and now needs to be justified. So why are you doing this for him? From the point of view of reducing offending and risk management, why are you doing that thing, that he will perceive as a goodie? To some extent, the baby's gone out with the bathwater. To another extent, one of the things people will not see that we've done for them, is we'll have referred to accommodation agencies while they're inside. They won't acknowledge that they went in dependent on methadone, their dosage has been maintained inside, and there's a treatment provider with a prescription waiting for them when they get out. And most people, local at least, get out on a Friday, because they were sentenced on a Friday. Hundreds of times I've seen colleagues on a Friday afternoon trying to find somewhere to live and a script for someone who's just got out. It's the classic scenario. We're not estate agents. We don't have keys. We have pretty good relationships with a number of organisations and no fucking influence with lots of others. The biggest landlord in any borough is the council. Only once, in my career of nearly thirty years, have we had a real functioning relationship with a council where we could get people places to live, with a package of support and a close working relationship with the cops.

Keith

You have to give people the skills to find work. Housing is a massive issue, because so many have chaotic lives and getting back into housing is often a real problem. We tried to get local authorities to accept the fact these people belong in their area, they're going to come back there, so they've got to take some responsibility. But councillors are voted in locally and there's big public pressure on them, with people asking why they're giving ex-prisoners flats when they're on the waiting list. If somebody goes out and they've got a steady relationship that's a positive influence on them, if they've got somewhere to live, a job, they're far less likely to offend. That's a simple truth we've known for years, but actually being able to deliver that seems impossible and I don't know why. We need to take a long hard look at how we work with offenders, rather than just changing things every five years when we have a change of government. We've got to find a solution, otherwise people will still go round this revolving door of offending, prison, back out, offending, prison.

Stephen

I don't see any logical reason why we couldn't take the prison population back down to levels in the early nineties. That's still pretty high by European standards, and that's halving it. People aren't inherently more criminal now. Some groups have grown disproportionately, such as sex offenders, with more active policing, better cultures of reporting, technology and DNA. I don't have complaints about sex offenders going to prison, I think that's the right default position. But putting women in for shoplifting is just mad, and some men don't need to go to prison, there's other things we could do to work more effectively.

Gary

Some people are proud because their first child went to University. My first born went to prison instead. When he gets out, there'll be me, his girlfriend, his mam, his brother. Even if he doesn't want to travel back with me, I'll be there when he walks through those prison gates. It will be like him being born again, a proud moment for a dad. I'll always back him up. He's done wrong, but he's my son.

Craig

You see all those programmes with people coming out and somebody waiting for them. But I said to mam, let us get settled and I'll get in touch. It's hard to sink in, what it's like getting out. Everything in prison is walking pace, then suddenly I'm in a car on a dual carriageway with all these trees flying past. I was trying to listen to what they were telling me but I couldn't take it in. Staff in the hostel were pretty similar to prison, all the rules and that, the only difference was I could leave. But when I first went out I only took about ten steps and I had to stop and calm meself down, there was too many people. And in prison, everyone's walking one way, then when they come back they're all walking the other way. Suddenly I've got people walking left, right and centre, it was frightening. I haven't the paranoia I had when I first came out, but I never leave me road the same way and I come back from different directions, and I keep expecting someone to be following us. If I hear a van pull up outside, I'm sure it's a police van. I don't like to look smart either, I try to blend in, and I usually go out on the day when it's nice and quiet and come back on the night. Now I'm out,

I have PPU, the Public Protection Unit. I was seeing her every Tuesday because I was doing this Better Life course, but now I have to go to the police station and see her. She asks what I've been doing and I tell her. I have to tell her if I start a relationship. She doesn't tell me what to do or give me advice, she just keeps a check on me.

Caroline

I got seconded from the field team to the hostel, what they call 'approved premises,' and I worked there for nearly four years. They used to be bail hostels. People who couldn't go home because of domestic violence were bailed there, but they take high risk MAPPA offenders who've been in custody now, who are coming out on licence and are potentially too risky to live within the community unsupervised, either that or sex offenders who haven't completed the programme because they haven't admitted their offences. The hostel has twenty three people, six females and seventeen males. The building's purpose built, people come out of prison and say it's just like being back there, except they can walk out the door, as long as they're back by curfew. And it's really strict, if they're not in at 11pm the front door's locked, and if they come at one minute past the police are rang and they're potentially recalled. It's rare for anyone to be recalled for not coming back by curfew time though, because the majority have long licences and are predominantly sex offenders and paedophiles and they're really compliant within the rules structure. It's only the odd one that has drug and alcohol issues and so is chaotic because of that. Usually, you ask them to do something and they do it, they play the game. They're not allowed mobile phones, they're not allowed computer access or to go to public libraries because they have computers there. They're not allowed to live close to schools, so that makes housing difficult, and if you don't work closely with housing you push people underground, they disappear, and you don't know where they are and that's far more dangerous. I'd rather have a really compliant sex offender next door to me than some bloody drug dealing gangster, honestly.

Antonio

Layla puts a hand on her husband's shoulder and smiles. I said to
the Probation Officer, it's a long way, we're never gonna get there before half three on a Friday. She said, I'm looking at a hostel, bring him
there, stop a couple of times, get summat to eat, I'll see you when you
get there, but don't take the piss, I want to go home. We landed half
seven at night didn't we? We had loads of stops.

Antonio laughs and shakes his head. She was desperate to go home,
which we'd planned. I'd never met her before in my life, after nearly
thirteen years in prison, and she hadn't a clue who I was. She didn't
realise she was dealing with a high security Category A prisoner, she
thought she was dealing with just some normal release. Ten days later,
she read my file and thought, oh my God. They didn't tell me, she said,
I didn't realise. She changed the whole parameters of our relationship
then. But imagine if I was some kind of dangerous axe-murderer? She
didn't even turn up for the first two appointments.

Craig

I was absolutely shitting meself. I heard this little voice, hiya son,
and I turned round. Me mam must have shrunk, she seemed half the
size, and I didn't know what to do but she gave us a hug. I see her
three times a week now, and she's admitted she used to come just to
check up, but now she comes because she wants to, and that's a big
thing for me. We sat in the hostel for two days. She asked all the questions she wanted, I told her every detail and we got it all over with. She
still won't talk about the past, but we're getting on better than we ever
have. I've had four dads over the years, and I see none of them now.
Our relationship went down when I found me real dad and told her.
She hit the roof, called me all the bastard trouble causing cunt under
the sun. We've got a family funeral this Wednesday. Me aunty brought
us up more than me mam did, and she died last week. I gave our Billy a
card and said, out of respect I'll stay away. I don't want them to have a

funeral and worry about what's going to happen. If you want us there, then let us know, but if I don't hear from you I'll stay away.

Donna

They brought agencies in where you referred on for accommodation, and the thing I can't stand the most is there's nowhere for them to live. You see someone inside for sentence planning and they say, I've nowhere to live, and so you fill all the forms in and get everything off, and they come out and say, I've nowhere to live, and you say, yeah, I know, because the hostel places are all used up for high risk. I've had loads of instances where I couldn't get them anywhere, so they became homeless and had to go to the council every day, and hopefully get a bed and breakfast or be sofa surfing, either that or I've bought them a tent or sleeping bag out of my own money. This one feller lost his fingers and toes with frostbite, it was horrible.

Keith

There's a report from 2003, something Tony Blair set up, the Social Enquiry Forum, looking at reasons people offend. They identified seven key pathways. Several areas were heavily involved with local authorities to try and develop this approach, so there wouldn't be this gap between someone leaving prison and not being able to move into accommodation. East Midlands was a particularly good example and the impact upon re-offending was tremendous. But we do this, and then someone else comes along in the Ministry of Justice and decides they wants to change things. Who's encouraging the local authorities to take this approach to crime reduction and community safety now?

Stephen

Budgets focus on full prisons but not full community sentences. Let's say there are 250,000 people being supervised on community sentences now, by a certain number of staff; if that becomes full it's not noticed in the same way as a prison becoming full is. Now let's say there were forty-four thousand prisoners in 1992, and I'm not far out there. If the money to take that up to another forty thousand, which is eventually what we've done, was instead moved to Probation, then Probation would feel like a hugely overfunded service, they'd have so much money they wouldn't know what to do with it. That's because once you put funding into a residential service, the cost goes up massively. Making any part of the punishment residential drives cost and pulls money away from other areas.

Val

They wanted me in a hostel. I had my own house but they wouldn't put me there because I'd threatened to kill my ex and his family, so they kept me in a few months longer. My Probation Officer forgot about me and went on holiday, but she must have referred me because I got this lovely flat. I had two of my girls with me and the landlord put this banner up that said welcome to your new home. I can't put it into words, what it was like seeing my girls when I got out. My oldest girl stuck by her husband who's stabbed her. His family smashed all my windows when I got out, because it's the same family as my ex. Seeing my other girls was amazing. But then I was homesick, because I never had any security in my flat, I was homesick for jail. If I could have took the kids in there, everything would have been alright.

Rebecca

Nathan went to the local prison before he was released, they don't release from high security. He ended up in a cell with my brother, and they hadn't seen each other for thirteen years. My brothers and sisters, they never saw Nathan. His cousins, they never saw Nathan. Because they said Cat A, only certain people can see him, and they have to go through vetting procedures. So in fifteen years of prison, Nathan has seen about ten people he knew from outside. And if I was putting hours together, all the time I've seen Nathan in the past fifteen years, even since he's been out, I couldn't say I've seen him for a week. He comes round and says he's staying for the weekend, but he drops his bags and he's gone. Then he comes to pick his bags up, puts them in the car and he's gone again.

Do you think he feels guilty about putting you through so much?

I don't know. I think so. *There's a long pause.* You know, sometimes you don't even know it, you think you're fine, but really you're depressed.

Sophie

I can be a little needy sometimes, and demand peoples full attention because I need to know they're always there. I've been with my boyfriend for four years now though, so I have got a lot better. But I'm very insecure at times and deep down that must have something to do with my dad. The main feeling is rejection. I just wish I had a normal dad that was around and loved me like my other friends' dads.

Caroline

There's lots of judgement made about offenders, all kinds of offenders, because you don't like what they've done and you'll probably never understand the offences they've committed. But you've signed up to work with them, so you have to do what you can to address risk. Some of the hostel team were good but some were awful and on a power trip. This one female bullied staff and residents. If residents had an issue, she'd say, why's that my problem? Sort it yourself, I'm busy. She had massive mental health issues, and in Probation, it's amazing how many people have, honest, I think it attracts people with issues and I don't know why. There's a lot of people in this line of work, right across the criminal justice system, prison, police, probation, even some social workers to a degree, it's cathartic for them. And I don't think you can ever go into this type of work in that mind-set, doing it for the wrong reasons, because your sins will find you out sooner or later. You're not doing anybody any justice or service, including yourself.

Colin

I was nervous, very nervous. It was the unknown, and there was an enormous amount of fear about being able to stay out and not get recalled. I got moved to a hostel forty miles from friends and family, and I think that was deliberate to keep me more controlled and isolated. They do a course called Footsteps. It's about positive thinking but it was designed for companies and then tailored to people who've been released from prison. I had to attend a couple of times a week in a group. It was worthless. Nobody wanted to be there and some were falling asleep. Hostel staff just monitor and that's it. You get no help whatsoever towards housing, and no help finding bonds if you need them. You have a weekly meeting, maybe twice a week. They ask if your licence has been adhered to and that's it.

Craig

Probation in the hostel do nothing, and I mean absolutely nothing. You have two meetings a week, on Mondays and Fridays. Is there any issues? No? Right then, fill your diaries in, show you've been productive. I honestly haven't had any help from them whatsoever. Everything I've done, throughout prison and afterwards, I can't see where they've done anything, apart from suggest the odd course. These probation hostels, they call them approved premises now, they have between twenty and thirty lads and they're always full. You have to communicate with people inside, otherwise they say you're being anti-social. But the second you get out you're not allowed to. If I'm going in the same direction, I can't even walk with them because it's classed as associating. There's this lad who wants to change his name but he's shite on a computer. I did it online, so I said I'd meet him in the library and show him, but he needs to get approval from the Public Protection Unit and that keeps us both in the clear.

Peter

Everyone convicted of sex offences nowadays will be registered. They get visits from the Public Protection Unit, and if they're not at their address then they will go and look for them, and they'll be prosecuted. What I know is; you need to worry a lot less about the ones you know about, because they're pretty well managed.

Val

The thing with jail is, you've got a beginning and a middle, but you've no fucking end. There's this constant cycle of people and when they get out, they're shot on the street. They go, oh, we'll help you with your housing, we'll do this, we'll do that, and they do fuck all. They said to me, right Valerie, what courses would you like to do? I said, are you fucking real? I've got no leccy, I've got no gas, there's no blankets on the beds. They said, with an attitude like that, you'll be going back. I said, with an attitude like that, you can fuck off. There's just no end. And they never helped with the leccy, gas and blankets, but I worked for this woman in a gym when I was in the open prison, and she got my address. They're not supposed to give addresses out, but she must have got it off someone, and she was worried because one minute I was there and the next I wasn't. She sent me five bags of food from Iceland. My daughter said, can we really choose anything from these bags? I said, yes darling, you can. Because before that, we were stealing food together, we had pockets full of cheese and bacon.

Sophie

I don't speak to my dad at all now. I sometimes feel sorry for him but I don't understand why I should. Most of the time I just don't even want to think about him.

Rebecca

Errol's in prison now. And just before Nathan came out, Rishi went inside. He came out two months ago. There's so much ups and downs. I've got them, then they're inside and I've got their children. When Nathan went in, this girl Claire was pregnant with his baby. Nathan said, when the baby's born, I want you to go see her, and it's my grandchild and I hadn't even met Claire, so I went and this girl's mum didn't help, she went to Scotland. Claire got a flat in the area I was living in, and I had the little girl every day, then one day she just took the child and left, she didn't say nothing. And I don't really know what to talk about because it's all been, just difficult. *She pauses.* Rishi's been shot. And some of the stories, some things that happened, I don't know why they happened, because my children are not secretive, but even with Nathan and the shooting of a police officer, he hasn't sat down with me and said, mum, this is what happened. I was at court but I've never heard his story. I asked when he came out, but he said, you don't need to know that. I wanted to spend one day, just one day, to sit down with him. We haven't had that day yet, and I understand because it's stressful for him. He's lost weight, he's had diarrhoea, and I don't know the full term affect prison's had on him.

Licence

Colin

I've been out six months, this time around. I came out in 2014, was out eight months, then got recalled for another ten. I'd got straight back into work. I'm a wagon driver by trade, and I needed a medical, a digi card and my CPC, eighty-five hours of compulsory training. But I needed funding for it and no help was available from Probation, so I found a place, through my own investigation, a company that helps. They asked me down for an interview. I made my way there on a push-bike in the pissing rain and was only allowed to do it at the last minute because Probation threatened to recall me if I attended the meeting, because I hadn't been cleared for that particular library the interview was being held at. They were actually going to recall me for going for funding for getting back to work. But I phoned two different supervisors, got clearance and hot-footed it down there. Then I had to fight through curfews to attend the training, I had to run back to the hostel every time, because I had to be back by four and Probation refused to shift the curfew an hour. Then they charged full rent and housing benefit in the hostel, so I had to find somewhere else to live, and I was desperately trying to save money to get a bond but they were taking more off me. I managed it, but when I got recalled I lost everything. I was given another phone for work, and stupidly, I neglected to tell Probation, so it cost me nearly a year in prison. I lost the job, the flat and everything in it, including the furniture.

Daniel

I needed a job and I knew the country needed lorry drivers, so I passed my licences. Probation said, we need to talk to your employer and tell them about your licence and crime. I said, well nobody's going to fucking employ me then, are they? It's part of your licence conditions, they said. And I'm not high risk here, I'm back down to medium risk. So I started a limited company, a transport company. I said, there's the number, I'm VAT registered, there's all my company accounts, I'm renting myself out to other companies. Well we need to talk to these other companies. Why? I don't work for them. My licence conditions state you need to talk to whoever employs me. I'm the managing director. I'll tell you exactly where I'm going anytime you want. It got to the point where I had to ring them up and tell them the model and registration number of every lorry I got in, and where I was going. I left it on their answer-machine and they wrote it down, every one. So one day I said to the boss, can I do some shunting for a few days? I fancy a change. Shunting's where you get into a truck, move the trailer, get into another truck, move the trailer. I got into sixty trucks that night. Probation rang me four days later and said, you're doing this for your own amusement, I don't believe you got into all those trucks. I went into my next meeting with pictures of every truck I'd got into, and the number plates. I explained what shunting was and she said, okay, we don't need that now, we trust you. And so they go off my tachograph instead, because it put their noses out of place and created too much work.

But look at that from Probation's point of view. Were they not doing that to ...

Protect the public? Were they fuck. How can they protect the public by doing that? I said to them, I get in my car, I don't have to tell you where I'm going. I get in my mates car, I don't have to tell you the registration number. It doesn't make sense. They were doing it to throw me off, because if I wanted to commit crime, I'd have done it with a mate wouldn't I? And people get recalled to prison so easy. For the first three or four months, they actually want to recall you, I promise. Say you've got nine dogs to control, would it be easier to control them locked in a pen or running around a field? I know someone who got recalled for being twenty minutes late for an appointment. They got recalled for 28 days. I know someone that went round his wife's house when her new boyfriend was in, and he wasn't supposed to be near this boyfriend, but he went there to pick the kids up at the time they told him to pick the kids up. He got recalled for that. And I wouldn't get a standard recall, I'd get three months, and my licence doesn't finish until 2024. I can't go on holiday, I'm not allowed to leave the country, not allowed more than five grand in my bank unaccounted for, not allowed more than five hundred in my pocket, not allowed any mobile apart from the one I've got. Any car I own, I have to give them my number plate. Any relationships, I have to tell them who my girlfriend is. I'm not allowed to reside out for one night without permission. If they tell me to do another stupid course and I say no, they'll recall me, whatever the impact on my work. There's that many conditions you actually forget what some of them are.

Paige

My youth offending workers were mint. We used to go to churches and paint them. We went to workshops and made bird hutches. That was awesome. This one woman took me to the doctors and the dentist. But it all changes when you get older. And when I came out of prison it was just a few weeks before my eighteenth birthday so they changed me over to Probation.

Colin

This ridiculous dance goes on. Where have I been going? She already knows because of my tag. What have I been doing? Who have I been speaking to? My sons live up North, and there's no restrictions on seeing my youngest son, my oldest son's my co-accused but my youngest son's not, and he's eighteen. I was planning a day trip up there and I mentioned I might meet him. My Probation Officer said she wouldn't approve home leave unless I agreed not to see him. She would stop me staying at my girlfriend's if I met my son. And there's no restrictions around him, she's just making things as difficult as possible. She wants to recall me, because then she can say she was right when she told the Parole Board she didn't want me out of prison. I'm not allowed to work and I've not been told what I can do to make myself suitable for work. I've signed on the sick, to keep money coming in and rent being paid, because the flat I've got is my approved premises, and if I lost that I'd get recalled. I've asked for overnight stays with my girlfriend but it's been refused. She said the relationship isn't stable enough yet. I've been with my girlfriend two years, we got together the last time I was out. She finds it enormously difficult and we've had conversations about me going back to prison and finishing my sentence, if that would be a better option. That's three years, but I get so much pressure off Probation, I see it as bullying. Ultimate power ultimately corrupts doesn't it? I've done everything they've put in front of me, she still obstructs work. I've got a flat with hardly anything in it, with floorboards instead of carpets. I could have been working from day one, but instead I go to food banks.

Gary

Jack will be on a four year licence when he comes out in sixteen months. If he didn't have a loving family he'd have to be in a bail hostel. It's going to be hard. I know the Probation Officer, I've worked with her. She's putting restrictions on him. He has to do a healthy relationships course but hopefully he can do that in prison. And social services will be involved because his new girlfriend has children.

Billy

I was on a tag and I had this younger Probation woman and she was an absolute twat. I had all these conditions because I was in a village where I'd committed crimes. I wasn't allowed in this street, I wasn't allowed past this fucking house. Within two days, I got this letter through, a warning from Probation saying I'd been seen through this street, and I hadn't been there, it was the grasses I'd been done for, trying to get me recalled. I phoned the woman and asked if she had proof. She hadn't. She said the police were supposed to have been to see me, but they hadn't. I went straight down the office. This woman was about thirty, with a proper bad attitude. She was a control freak and she didn't know how to speak to people. I said, you can't give me a warning without proof. She said, I can do what I want. She never once tried to help me. I fucking hated her. I said I want to change my Probation Officer because I've obviously upset you about something. She said, you can't. I ripped my tag off and got recalled. Looking back now, if I had a different Probation Officer, if I had that older woman who came to see me in prison, I probably wouldn't have got recalled. That woman was respectful. She made you feel like after prison, you could still have a future.

Keith

Relationships between prisons and Probation have always been a concern. Lots of good things went on in prisons, but there's this gap when someone's released back into the community and Probation take over. Offender Management has never worked effectively except in small examples. There's been some interesting pilots around the country, with multi-disciplinary teams of Probation, Police, Housing etc. focused on prolific offenders, the PPO Scheme. That went back to the original basis of what Probation was about, helping people who've had difficult lives going back into the big world again. Some of those schemes worked really well, because we targeted individuals and gave them support to get their lives back together. They were around 2005, 2006, but like many Home Office backed things, they have a pilot and disappear into the shadows. In my women's prison, we had a fantastic scheme mentoring offenders when they left, and I've heard this is where CRC is falling down badly, because they haven't got the mentors in place.

Donna

I went to see this man and I was telling him what would happen when he started up his mouth, and God, he was horrendous. He went mad. I got up and said, do that to me? Like you think I'm bothered. Every time you're out, I'll get you recalled. He got hauled off shouting and screaming about what he was going to do to me. Anyway, he comes out and he has to meet me. And I said, start on, and I promise you, what did I tell you? He said, you know what? You're the first person that's ever been straight with me and I know where I am with you. And from that day on, I worked with the lad, I got him a job and I got him settled. He did his licence and played the game because he said I was bothered enough to stand up to him, and he thought, well if she's bothered to do that, I'll bother with her. I managed to do work on his drinking, all these things that had never been touched before. I'd tell him, I've told you, don't start with me. He'd say, yeah, I know, and he'd come back and we worked as a team. He always said, if you need me, get in touch. And word goes out, in prison and on the out, if you treat somebody alright, it would be, she's alright her.

Craig

Everything can be done in stages, a little bit at a time. I learnt that in creative writing and art, thinking what would work best in each situation. I sit down and plan it. And because I'm not worried now about going up to people, and I'm always pleasant and straight to the point, it works an awful lot. When I came out, I realised Probation weren't going to help us get me own house, and I heard of this support group that helps vulnerable people, but I was back to how I was when I first went to jail, scratching and nervous. Being in prisons and hostels, you're answering to somebody, you've got to be in by a certain time, you've got to do this, you've got to do that. Then suddenly I had to do things for meself. But I had the confidence to say what I needed, I was honest and open, it went fine and they found us a place. Probation wouldn't let us move in though, there was a school within a mile radius. They found us another place but Probation wouldn't let us move there either, there was a private nursery a few streets away. I would have festered over it before, got meself worked up, blamed the system and everybody else. But I just got on with it and eventually it came right down to me last day. I was all packed up, ringing round hostels to find a bed for the night, when that support group got in touch and said they'd found somewhere. I looked at it and loved it. There was no furniture and I was scared to put the radiators on because I didn't know how much it would cost, but the support group got us some furniture, a table and chairs and a bed. And then I went into a library and used me IT skills to put me name down for other household things.

Caroline

I worked with one man who'd come out of prison, and he'd only got four years, but he came out on an extended licence for fifteen years. His offences were horrendous and numerous, he'd targeted women with little boys and groomed the mothers to get to the sons, and he was in total denial so he couldn't do the programme. I made it my mission to make him admit what he'd done. We used Crown Prosecution Service packages, witness and victim statements. We read through them and fed them to the offender and said, right, this is what your victim's saying, what's your view? I made notes and compared them to his original statements. I did this for years and he kept saying, I didn't do it. Just before I left for maternity leave, I said to him, this is the situation, I know you did it, the courts know you did it, your victims know you did it, you know you did it. All you've got to do is admit it, we've been through this for years. I was getting so frustrated with him. And then he broke down and cried, and he'd never cried before. He went for a cigarette, came back and admitted everything. And that's really important in reducing risk, acknowledging you've actually done something. He was more dangerous not admitting. Plus it makes it much easier for those working with him, because when someone's in total denial, especially with sex offences, you can't work with them. We had quite a good working relationship until that point and then he wouldn't talk to me at all, but he went on to do the Sex Offender Treatment Programme. I still see him now in Morrison's where I live, and when he sees me he runs and hides behind shelves.

Gary

Jack said his Probation Officer was quite nasty to him. I met her and she seemed hyper and a bit arrogant. But people told her I used to work in that office as a Probation Service Officer, that I know the system. And ever since then she's been on the phone to Jack asking if there's anything she can do for him.

Colin

What have I learned? Don't trust Probation. My recall was way in excess of what should have happened, given I wasn't doing anything wrong, other than having an extra phone and accessing normal internet sites with it. Maybe a warning, but an immediate recall? At my next parole hearing, my Probation Officer was the only one that didn't want me released, she wanted me inside for another year. I think that's why she's making things as difficult as possible for me now. I've had a job offer from day one, but my licence conditions state I can only take up work that's approved by her, and at the moment she doesn't approve anything. She wanted me to do a disclosure to my employer, which they'd already had because I'd worked for them the last time I was out. They told her they didn't want or need a disclosure. She said they had to give it, in her presence, but they're based on the other side of the country. I tried to negotiate. They said they'd find time for a three-way telephone conference, but she said she wouldn't believe it was them on the other side of the phone, even though I'd arranged she could ring them. She won't let me use computers at the Jobcentre either. I spoke to an organisation who said there is no legislation stating you have to disclose past offences, it's only if a company requires you to. So Probation are breaking the law and I've asked her in writing to tell me what legislation she's using to force disclosure on an employer that doesn't want it. But she refuses to answer in written form, she'll only say verbally she doesn't agree.

But she'll argue it's on your licence conditions, and therefore it's part of your licence.

It's not on my licence conditions to disclose to employers because it can't be. It's on my licence that she has to approve any work, it's vague enough for her to do what she wants. Legally speaking there's no requirement for me to disclose past offending, if they don't wish it. If they ask, I have to tell them and be truthful, but if they don't want to know, or they already know, which is the case in mine, it's not necessary.

Peter

Management, team management particularly, was more about nurturing workforce than measuring and monitoring them, and that's just a redistribution of resources, it's not new ones. Now, there's a culture of criticism that makes us risk averse and defensive practitioners, but thank God there are people brave enough and with enough integrity to put their signature on a piece of paper that says, the balance of probability is, and that's all it is, the balance is this can be managed in the community. These are old figures, but under the old Discretionary Conditional Release system, ninety-seven percent of parole licences were successfully concluded. It's probably higher now because we're much more selective about who gets parole. It's one thing to get a standard recall of twenty-eight days, some people like drug users will run that risk, but when you've done a long sentence and you could go back for an indeterminate time, people aren't going there. And in terms of serious further offences, Schedule 15 offences that occur by people on supervision or within thirty days of its completion, eighty percent came from low to medium risk.

Rebecca

I got my friend to drive me up to the hostel, three or four days after Nathan was out, because it's nearly one hundred miles away, and he was like, what are you doing here? You shouldn't be here. My nephew wanted to drop him something off but he's so paranoid they'll recall him. Even now I think to myself, any little thing and he could be gone again. And now Rishi has come out, he actually looks up to Nathan, but they put Nathan so far away. And Rishi's not allowed to have contact with his other brother that's in prison. What kind of thing is that? How do we go on as a family? He's not allowed to have contact with his nephew and his brother. I mean, his brother's a criminal if that's the way the law's looking at it, and he's a criminal, but it's not like he's a good boy and the brother's the criminal who's going to influence him. It's not like they've been in trouble together so they need to be apart, their crimes are separate. So when they do these things, you ask yourself, what is there to gain? The punishment never stops.

Gary

The victim's moved to the same street Jack's grandma lives on, and Probation's told us he won't be able to visit her. I spoke to his solicitor and he said, we'll sort that out nearer the time. What would happen if the victim moved into my street? My son wouldn't be able to visit me?

Paige

The Probation Officer was snobby, she was stuck up her own arse and she looked down on me as if I was nothing. So I kept complaining and I got a new one, and this new one gave me bus fares and was much better.

Colin

I've seen lads purposely getting recalled because of the pressure they were under, the restrictions and lack of help. They decided to go back to prison to finish their licence, so they didn't have Probation on top of them when they got released again. It's easier to do all your licence in prison, particularly on short sentences. I saw a group of five lads purposely go off on a bender for a few days in order to get recalled.

Peter

I don't think it's true that Probation want to recall people. I can see, in a general way, why that rationale makes sense, but doing recall papers is a piece of fucking work. The cops love recall. They ring you up and say, so and so's out, we've had a spike in domestic burglaries, will you recall him? And we say, give us a charge sheet with an offence for which they'd go to jail, then I'll recall him. If the cops bring me a convincing charge sheet, I'll spend a good four hours on recall papers, and I'm pretty quick, and I'm not doing other stuff I need to do, because by nature recall is an emergency. People are categorised as recall with twenty-four hours, or recall within two hours, so the clock's ticking straight away. Your manager reads the forms, accepts them or suggests amendments, puts his or her signature on it, then sends it to their manager, who also goes through them. Then they go to the Home Office, and if it's a two hour recall, the senior manager sits by the phone to see they've been picked up, or puts a contingency plan in place. So that's not easy, it doesn't make your life simple. It may the day after, when they're locked up, but in many cases you've done all that for a twenty-eight day recall and they come out again bitter and twisted.

Daniel

I've got a different Probation Officer now mine's left. I go in every four weeks. He asks me loads of questions, I say yes, no, yes, no, then leave. The Probation Officer that left was alright. After the first three months, she actually said to me, I now believe you want to change your ways, and since then she bent over backwards to help me, she were brilliant. But it took her three months to believe me, and surely she should have wanted to help me from day one and took the gamble. I said to her all the time, why don't you help me? She said, do you know how many people have said this to me? I said, look, it's your job. Even if a hundred people say this to you, and only two turn out to be genuine, you've done your job. You shouldn't be there to trip people up. She said, my first job is to protect the public. My second is to help you.

Valuing The Sinner

John

If you're doing your fifth, sixth, seventh prison sentence, some-thing's not right somewhere. Look at *why* they're coming back. One gets out on a Friday, puts a brick through the supermarket window and comes back on the Saturday. But others aren't like that, they have stuff outside, and the day you would rather be in prison than outside is a day that needs examining. You can't phone your mam, or be there for your daughter's birthday. You can't pop out to McDonalds. Little things. If you want a crap during the night and you haven't got toilet roll, you've got to ask someone and they might take an hour on pur-pose. This chap who works in a kiosk in the town, who does the keys and shoe repairs, he said, it must be easy being in prison, you've got everything you want. I said, Friday, when they shut the town centre, I'll bring you a telly, I'll put it on that little shelf there and you sit in there 'til Monday. Your kiosk's the same size, you've got a telly, if it's good enough for them, you won't mind over the weekend, they're doing five, ten years in there. I'd hate to be on the other side of the door. People tell me prison's easy, they've got PlayStations, they've got tellies. They have no idea. Until you're on the other side of the wall, and I'm telling you, no you can't go to the toilet and no, you can't phone your mum, even though she's ill. I never said no without giving a reason, but some officers do and just walk off. People have no idea what it's like.

Adele

The amount of lads going out and coming back in, I don't think prison does work. Otherwise we wouldn't have so much re-offending would we? There's not enough for them to do. They're not supported enough when they get out, they're given forty-seven pounds, then they don't have any money for a month or two while they're sorting benefits out. If you've got nothing, what are you going to do? Self-preservation, isn't it? If they haven't got a home, a family, a positive network to support them. I couldn't manage on that money. Most of them have to go to a hostel as part of their bail conditions, or their licence or tagging. And these hostels are where they'll pick up with people and get back on the drugs straight away, even though they'll go out and have all these plans. I've had lads back in prison after a fortnight out, when the money's gone and they've robbed. And in winter, you get a huge influx because it's better than sleeping on the streets. At least they've got a bed, a bit of stability, a reason to get up in the morning, even if they're complaining about it all. It's a sad state of affairs isn't it?

Keith

We need proper resources in place. We need CRC mentoring programmes to have enough money. I was a trustee for a charity that recruited volunteer mentors that looked after people, took them for interviews for housing or employment, kept them occupied, and that had a beneficial effect, and a lot of that funding came from Probation. Then they went through that crisis of identity, say 2007, and all the money disappeared and went elsewhere. And some of those charities that were being really successful couldn't survive anymore, including the charity I was involved with. It's a great pity. A little bit of investment pays off in the long run.

Alice

You have to have prisons, of course, and we do need to protect the public. But the whole notion of a prison, and what it is, should be revolutionised. I was listening to Radio 4 the other day, about some women in a London prison being let out to go to college. One woman who'd been heavily involved in drugs, in crime and burglary, she was sent out Monday to Friday to do a year long course, and she lived at home so she could be with her kids, and then she came back to prison at the weekends. She's now got two businesses going. She was a business mind waiting to happen, but she never had the opportunities before.

And now she helps other women in prison, on similar schemes, adjust to being outside for the week. When her course finished, she was back inside to serve her final two and a half years, but she was planning her business for when she got out. Now that's amazing. She complied with everything because it was her chance to go down a positive avenue, she was learning skills and getting to see her kids. We have to work more with people, it's not all or nothing.

Sarah

It's a vicious circle. People are in there, out for two weeks and then back in. One guy gets released, goes over the road to ASDA and pinches a telly so he can be back the same day, because it's better than sleeping on the streets. I know it sounds harsh, but to me it should be that bad you'd never want to go back. They're like, see you on my next sentence Miss. What's up with these people? You see them when they're eighteen and they're still coming back in their thirties. There was a lot of courses at first, to help people with alcohol and drug addiction, but the courses were cut down as well as staff. And people were going in there who'd never touched drugs in their life, and by the time they got out they were addicted. The system's not working, obviously. And it's too easy for them. You can have a PlayStation 2 if you're enhanced, it has to be an old one because they don't have USB ports. You can shop in Argos, have catalogues and buy clothes, it's like home from home. In the past you could have clothes, books and CD's sent in, but then the prison stopped that and made contracts with companies to make more money. Prisoners had Sky television at the start, and that wasn't a privilege, that was standard. They paid 7p a day for it, including their television. People out here have to pay sixty pounds a month, they can't afford it. But they got rid of Sky, so it must have been costing the prison too much. It was a standing joke, people couldn't believe they got all those privileges. And they've put landline phones into cells now, whereas before you had them on the landing and they'd be queuing up like HMP. But that's the biggest money-maker, they earn thirty thousand a week off prison phones. They charge so much that ten pounds of credit goes in two days, even quicker if you're calling mobiles, that's one of the main reasons mobiles get smuggled in.

Peter

What are prisons for? Clearly they're to punish, and you would think as part of that punishment, they should deter. But we know people coming out of prison are more likely to re-offend than not. Any look at stats demonstrates that. So in terms of deterrents, it would appear they're not very good. If they're there to punish, you'd have thought the harsher the regime, the less likely they are to come back. But what we know is, the harsher the regime, the greater the depravation of liberty, which is supposed to be the punishment in the first place, the more likely they are to re-offend. So they're not very good at that either. They're there to protect the public. Well, unless we include prisoners and prison officers in the definition of public, and I really think we ought, then they're pretty good at that. They remove people from most of us, although as I've said, they make those individuals more likely to create victims when they come back out again. In terms of bullying and random acts of violence, in terms of drug dealing, extortion, intimidation of families, incidents of prison officers being assaulted, intimidated, stressed to the point of heart-attack, in terms of the extreme of homosexual rape, it's not a panacea; that myth of putting them on an island and all will be well.

Stephen

We have women prisoners in for shoplifting, it's barking mad. Instead of spending a five figure sum looking after a woman prisoner, those costs could be transferred to provide that individual with appropriate support, then they'd thrive and contribute to society in a positive way, instead of taking them out of society and taking their kids off them.

Caroline

They brought in national standards, then timescales on supervision plans, risk assessments and reviews. But there was flexibility at first. Then, all of a sudden it was, if you don't hit these targets, you'll be taken to capability, and if you don't hit them the next time you might go through the process of losing your job. But you can arrange a session in your head, write it all out and know exactly what it is you're going to do, then they walk in with an immediate crisis, like they've got no food or they've had their benefits sanctioned or they're getting evicted the next day, and all your plans go out the window. But if you don't hit that target you're getting taken to work capability and could be disciplined. So officers do work they have to do rather than work the client needs. I won't do that and I got into trouble with my manager, but I didn't sign up to be a data-inputter and it's become a lot about that, and consequently Probation staff have very little time to spend with people. And what constructive work can you do if you've got to spend all your time inputting data?

Donna

We had huge caseloads back in the day, but we saw prisoners and did the work ourselves because we didn't have bizarre assessments you had to spend hours on a computer on. Sometimes I would visit a prison on my day off, but I didn't mind, because I got so much out of it. It was a way of life, it wasn't just a job, it was who you were. And then I watched over the years as that wasn't valued, and I don't care about saying this, but people would be putting anything down on these assessments. You'd meet the lad in prison or out on licence and he'd say, I haven't done that work, I don't even know what you're talking about. It looked bloody marvellous on this assessment but the real work just wasn't getting done. And a lot of that was the change in mentality of the people coming in. A lot of the staff were actually frightened of the offenders. And I'm not blasé, I know about risk and I know how to protect myself, but Christ, if you can't build up a relationship you can never do the work. You might look at an offence, say a sex offence, and think God, how can a person do that? But if you don't work past that and get to the crux of it, how can you actually do the work? How can you reduce the risk?

John

Our jail went from four wings to seven, from six hundred men to over a thousand. All the government policies over those twenty years about reducing prison sentences and the population's doubled. And they don't all deserve to be in there, absolutely not. If your sentence isn't longer than six months you shouldn't be in prison, it's pointless. We've people going out on a Friday and coming back on a Monday. We discharge them but don't clean their cells because we know they'll be back. The streets are scruffy. The town's scruffy. Don't send them into prison and spend millions doing it, have them outside doing community work. The short sharp shock doesn't work. You hear prisoners on their fifteenth sentence saying prison's easier now than when they first came in. Nothing puts people off prison if they're that type of person, it's an occupational hazard for them. And it's a structure for ninety per cent of the lads we get in, structure they haven't had before. Lads are coming in with their diabetes all over the place and we're providing three meals a day and a structured time to get medication. They're going out ten times healthier than they came in. It's outside that needs to change, not inside. How, I don't know, I'm not a politician, but to put someone in jail for a month, seriously, what's being achieved? Apart from mountains and mountains of paperwork.

Keith

We have some very good managers down at Prison Service headquarters, the likes of Michael Spurr and others, who have a positive view of where prisons should go, but they're obviously bound by resources they're given. We need a free hand without politicians chipping in all the time, such as Michael Howard changing the rules on home leave all of a sudden, because of one article in The Sun. I was a covering governor at an open prison at the time. We had catholic women going out for Sunday Service and they couldn't anymore, because they had to go through a whole series of risk assessments. Politicians don't realise the impact they have on individuals lives, and a service that needs some freedom to make things work.

Stephen

The drive towards larger prisons is financially driven, and the financial side of things shouldn't be the sole driver. There is a case for high security being in larger prisons, dispersed throughout the country in one or two key places. But the overwhelming majority of prisons should be far more linked into regional economies. The Local Enterprise Partnerships have money from government, are about regional infrastructure, investment and stimulating the economy. We should be distributing prisons in places where there is economic deprivation. Prisoners could be stimulating demand there. There are some industries in this country that cannot recruit people. The key is not always seeing things through a criminal justice lens. Smaller prisons are better, and if appropriate, prisoners should be able to work during the day and come back at night.

Peter

It's too simplistic to say most thieves wouldn't be stealing if they had jobs. There's truth to it, but many thieves aren't ready to work. They may say they want to, but they're saying that in ignorance of what being in work would entail. When I left school I worked in factories. The daft lads were pushing brushes and working in stores. They had jobs. They had a place. They had stories to tell about the weekend on a Monday morning. They had wages. I'm not saying they never offended and I'm certainly not saying they never got into fights on a night out, but when people had a place there was less persistence to their offending, less frequency to it, and it probably had less duration. We've moved away from an industrial base to service, we don't make things anymore. People who make things are unusual these days. Try and get someone to fit a shelf for you. There are no easy answers, and within that thing about consistency of delivery and minimum standards, which are desirable, there needs to be something that says, this is the package for this one, this is the package that recognises this guy does need this and doesn't need that. And that has to be professional opinion rather than drop down menus. It's that thing about approaching them as a person, that Christ-like thing about valuing the sinner whilst rejecting the sin. You've got to accord people some dignity. It doesn't mean you've got to admire them or respect what they've done, but it means you've got to recognise why they've done that thing. I think most people within it do, but the system isn't geared up to that level of complexity.

Alice

The prison authorities need to see the devastating effect imprisonment has on kids and family. Everything is linked. You've got to look at things differently and be open minded. It's necessary to protect the public, and I do think there needs to be a punishment element too. If I steal a pound, I should get a pound's worth of damage back, that's karma, it's how life works and how we learn. But rehabilitation is also necessary, and it's this model that needs to revolutionise the whole system. Really concentrated and focused meditation classes in prison have changed some prison populations. It's about opening the mind to prisoners being people, no matter what they've done. There is humanity in everyone and that's what you have to go for, that untainted bit of humanity that is always there as long as a person is alive.

The Bigger Question

Antonio

These mountains are my background, my local heritage and culture. I feel this strange affinity with them, as if this is where we all originated, and when it gets down to it, we'll be alright, we're strong. I was brought up here by the kids home, because in the seventies and eighties they felt, to get an unruly and unsociable kid in hand, they had to take him camping, abseiling and canoeing. There were so many great young volunteers, we had a fucking whale of a time. Those were the only pleasant memories in my orphan childhood. After that, homes were closed down, there wasn't enough money to send kids to idyllic places, they were warehoused in industrialised chemical boxes outside the city. It was the end of an idyllic period, for the social services of Great Britain. The Labour government and the coal industry were going under. Maggie Thatcher was crushing the unions. Economically, the country was in turmoil, so the orphanages, the charities and the charity cases like me, were obviously affected. So whether or not it was a good thing, psychologically proven or whatever, it was a well-intentioned thing that was costing money that would never get spent again.

Rebecca

The judges, people in authority, they've never experienced these things. Social workers have never had a child taken away from them, or a family member in trouble, so that when they go to work they can respect the person they're dealing with. All they do is look down on you, like you're a criminal too. My youngest son, his daughter got taken away, not because he abused her, because he got shot. I went to court and they ordered someone to take my family away, and because I'd been going to church fifteen years, when they wrote my reference, it was unbelievable. But the judge said, they didn't know you before, this is just what they know of you now. So he took my granddaughter and he gave her to a woman that was a prostitute and had court cases pending. And me, I'm at home, I'm a church goer. She's my flesh and blood. What is that woman going to teach my granddaughter, if she's an ex-prostitute? What is she going to teach her that I can't? They said, if I want contact with my granddaughter, I have to break relationships with my son. How can you choose between your grandchild and your son?

Sophie

I don't know anyone else that I'm close to that has been in prison and I hope I never have to deal with it again. I think people that haven't got much in life may believe they get treated well in prison, you know, somewhere to sleep, food, TV, clean water and things.

Craig

All the way through prison, Psychology were full of false promises. If you do this course, that will happen. You need to do this course, to be able to do that. Not one bit of it happened. I got something from the courses but it was nothing to do with them or their promises. I honestly can't see any good they've actually done. If you can go all that time without one argument or one nicking, you do all the courses, do everything totally correct and it still doesn't work, you still don't get no help when you get out, then it's not gonna work for anybody else. I'm glad I went to prison though, because things could have escalated and ended up nasty. I had no boundaries, no moral compass, no empathy. Prison gave us the opportunity to get help. But you've got to go in there totally honest and do your best. So prison's worked for us, but the staff haven't and Psychology haven't, and when I got out I found Probation haven't. Everything I've achieved, I can't say any of them helped. The outside support group helped, the council helped, with their community support, but all those in charge, who are sat back getting their wages for being part of the rehabilitation service, they're all getting their money but they're not doing anything for it. I mean that's quite an achievement, to go all those years through two locals and a high security jail and not get in one argument or get one nicking. If I'd had family and I'd left a wife and kids at home, I don't know if I'd have dealt with it as easy as I did. It's only because I didn't have anybody really, apart from me mam.

Billy

Prisons don't work. If anything prison made me worse. I went to jail and learnt so much. And it's not a massive deterrent, it gets a bit boring but it's not exactly a punishment, apart from being bored and not seeing your family. I couldn't do a big sentence though.

Gary

Jack's little brother hardly went out the house for two years. He was frightened and he'd put on loads of weight. I said, I'm here to protect you, let me help. He kept saying, I'm alright. But something must have clicked. I don't know if Jack's had a word with him, but he goes out now, he's started bodybuilding. My step-sons still don't talk about it all though.

Antonio

In high security, you're locked up on your own and you're only allowed out your cell about six hours a day. Layla worked out that in all the time I spent in prison, and this doesn't include the twenty-four hour bang-ups down the block, and I did a good few months block, maybe a year block, I did 120,000 hours of solitariness. And my point is, and the bigger question I believe is, what the fuck does society expect to get out of a human being by doing that? If there are psychological implications involved then they should be aware of what psychological damage they could be doing. I'm quite a resilient person and I've got a lot of armoury, mental armoury, but I was on my fucking knees many times. A lot of weaker men than me are smashing up, killing, attempting suicide, whatever, coming out like wrecks and shells of people. Does the punishment fit the crime? I was in for non-violent crime, I didn't hurt one person, although yes, there was a lot of money involved.

Val

You can't do anything unless you want to do it yourself. Nothing will work. I told them, your courses are a load of fucking crap. Half the lasses want drugs because they'd been talking about them all day. Rehabilitation courses don't work. Three quarters of my mates are back on drugs. All of them that went into jail for drugs are still on it. None of them have got jobs. And when you're doing a long time, you see people coming back again, time after time. And then they shot you back out on the street? What the fuck. It's only because they get money for doing them courses. When you're out on the streets they don't help you, you're on your own, it's back to survival.

You say prison doesn't work, but also that you miss it and feel homesick for it.

They took me away from my kids, that's why prison doesn't work for women. And the kids did a sentence with me, except they didn't get a place of safety. I used to say to my little one, if only I could bring you here, we'd be happy. And my middle girl, she'd gone down to five stone because of the drugs. One lass was in there because she was on licence and she stole a pint of milk because she wanted a cup of tea. But I was sent to prison for a reason. I'd have either killed someone or they'd have killed me.

Paige

Prison's worked for me, because I've never been back, but other people don't learn. I've got a few lad mates who come out and thieve for drugs, then go back in again. Prison's like a second home for them. They're on Meow Meow and M-Cat and they're just not bothered. And the stabbing that happened just up the road, obviously I'm mates with the lad that done it. He's down that prison where all the young ones rioted and took over, and he's on Spice there. He's never going to learn. Last time he come out he tried to throw acid over someone.

Daniel

My pals ring me from high security and it might sound selfish but I use them as a boost to myself, to think, God I'll never do that again. They use me as someone to talk to, somebody to send them a bit of money at Christmas and send photos in, and I use them to stay focused on what I need to do to stay out. The only time I'll go back to jail is if anyone hurts my family or someone I love, so I think certain prisons work, but it depends on the individual. High security worked for me because I realised what I had outside of prison. I realised I'd got a nice family, and they were suffering. When I came out, I surrounded myself with positive people, people that want to do well successfully and legitimately, and so I've become one of them. Get a baby duck, put it with loads of piglets and it thinks it's a piglet. If I'd surrounded myself with drug dealers I'd have become a drug dealer. Prisons should have a lot more after-care to help you, not hinder you, because as Winston Churchill famously said at the House of Commons, a jail sentence should be about rehabilitation, not retribution. And when I got out of prison and got put into a hostel, it wasn't there to help me, it was there to trip me up.

Antonio

While I was in prison the time before last, I don't know why but I had this inspired vision that I must bring light. So when I got out, I drove to this place where I grew up as a kid, and there are boulders bigger than cars, loads of them dotted around on the edge of this cliff. I touched every one and imagined a bright light coming into the planet from the universe, through the earth and through my hands. I was about twenty three, and from that moment on, my life rocketed into success, in comparison with general success stories. By the time I was thirty five I was financially in a real good position, and my soft powers, my abilities to get things done, which can't be calculated in a bank account, were phenomenal. And I can trace some of that back, maybe all of that back, to meditating in a prison cell. But I do believe that every human being has got similar innate energies he needs to access, whether it can be found in a prison cell or taking ecstasy in Ibiza. Everyone's got to find their own path. They've got to understand what the fuck they are, what they've got to do in this world, and that understanding is within them, they've just got to find it.

Does prison help find that thing? For the majority?

What was it Oscar Wilde said? The sweetest things. Fuck, what was it? The vilest deeds and poisoned things bloom well in prison air, it's only what's good in men that rots and withers there. That's what prison's like, for ninety-nine percent of its residence, even in this modern society of televisions in cells. I grew up going in and out of prison as a youngster. In those days it was harsh treatment and lots of confinement. It was pissing in a bucket, no sanitary facilities, washing out your bucket, no heating, no windows, screws on the take. And the screws used to have a mess, an officers mess where they drank, and it was in the fucking prison, so if you pissed a screw off in the morning, he went away at dinnertime with his buddies, they had a few pints and you were in fucking trouble in the afternoon, believe me. There wasn't any legal restraints then, what you call reasonable force. It was kick the fucking shit out of you, drag you bloody and bleeding and dump you naked in a strip cell. Now it's become a bit more civilised. Human rights law and riots changed things. They've got televisions, they've got kettles and the fucking lads are still crying like onions.

Billy

There wasn't much support when I went from Youth Offending to Probation. Youth Offending were great but once I turned eighteen, it was next to no support, nothing. You get out and you're back to square one, that's why everyone re-offends. Probation were crap. You'd ask for support but they couldn't give you it.

Gary

Jack's hiding stuff. He's telling us what we want to hear because he doesn't want to upset us. I'll get to know more when he comes out. He sees lots of violence and drugs, but he keeps away from it. He's never said he's been bullied, but I'll never know unless he tells me when he comes out.

Rebecca

A lot of people in prison are good people, and sometimes good people make mistakes and don't need the punishment they get to rectify their mistakes. Even if Nathan had come out a bit more youthful, he would have put that experience to good use, and I think a lot of men in prisons could do so much better if they gave them opportunities. But Social Workers, Probation Officers, they don't have life experiences, and before they think about looking after their clients, they think about losing their job. So no matter what that person does, even if they're on the right track, they're not thinking along that line, they're thinking this is a murderer or a robber, and I'm going to give him no chances because if I make a mistake then this is my job.

Planting Seeds

Peter

Crime is a fascinating thing, isn't it? There are some guys, not many of them, although that's measured in thousands rather than dozens, who really are functioning at their best in a high security wing. We've got cop shows and crime writers and still very little perception of the complexity for it and the reasons criminals go into it. Most people think criminals become criminals because the hours are short and they're printing money, but actually lots and lots of criminals are working very long hours for really shit money. John McVicar wrote, 'the biggest motivator of the professional criminal is the respect of his peers.' I think that's absolutely true, and it's true of an awful lot of us. He also wrote, and it's more true now than it was then, 'there are guys who'd rather put an inch on their biceps than take a year off their sentence.' And that was written when the gym culture didn't extend far out of high security. They're both aspects of the same phenomenon. We've inadequately prepared these people, in terms of their family of origin and their experiences as young people, in their experiences of education and society. We've not, for a variety of reasons, given them the equipment, and they've been unable to develop the equipment, to function as citizens.

John

Super Prisons, this talk of two or three thousand; that's turning it into a machine, a shameless factory. Six months or less shouldn't be a custodial sentence, I'm passionate about that, it's ridiculous and pointless. When things happen in town, you read a life for a life, lock them up and throw away the key. I'm not for any of that, it's absolute nonsense. Some of the nicest people I've looked after were murderers, we're all capable of it. I couldn't steal cars on a daily basis but I could lose my temper and hit someone, find myself in prison and suddenly

I'm a murderer. We need to reduce the prison population because the more people are in prison, they just turn into people factories. People say they're training grounds for criminals and there's an element of truth in that. If you're not a criminal and you spend six months on a wing then you can't help but adopt their ways, even if you don't want to. It's survival mode. When there's ten people having a go at a prison officer and one's standing back saying, it's nothing to do with me, then he's going to be targeted. So short sentences no, big sentences training, preparing them for getting out, rehabilitation one hundred percent. And prison officers should have a big hand in rehabilitation. These lads are there twenty-four hours, it's no good giving them intense input for six hours and then putting them behind their door for the other eighteen. Have prison officers on association, playing pool, doing courses with them the next day. You've got to involve officers with civvies, otherwise it doesn't work. You wouldn't have a team of nurses looking after a patient for six hours, then a team of porters looking after them for eighteen, so why do that with prison officers? I'm not saying you should have prison officers doing it wholly but involve them. So the future for me would be no short term sentences and integration between prison staff and civvie staff, and total rehabilitation. Don't keep prisoners locked in their cells, you might as well put them in a cattery or kennels if that's what you want to do.

Keith

We need a long term view of how we organise our criminal justice system. Government changes every few years cause changes in the direction and ethos of what prisons are all about. We need a long term strategy. Michael Gove talked about the rehabilitation revolution. Now Liz Truss has come in and said something totally different, that prisons should be tough. What do these things even mean? These politicians need to spend time inside a prison, to see what they're talking about, before they come out with such nonsense.

Alice

I made a big contribution as a teacher through the years, and that's good for me, because sometimes you have a picture of this grey, dull, concrete, steel jungle, that saps the life out of you, and you look back and think, God, why did I spend so long in there? And that mostly comes from the pressure you get from security, because it devolves you of all personhood at times. The only time things were alive were in the classroom.

Stephen

It's shameful we've not had more psychologists in young offenders institutions. All the evidence states that's where we're likely to have the most results. I've worked with a governor in high security who then went to a young offenders institute and he said, I've no resources anymore. They need to focus far more on young offenders. Let's suppose that something we do works, and it works with a twenty-one year old rather than a forty-two year old, there's a lot more return on the public for that. But twenty five percent of psychological services are put into high security, just five or six prisons out of more than one hundred, that's a ludicrous distribution of services, absolutely indefensible. High security is over resourced and there's too many staff, but that's against the popular narrative. They also have many prisoners that are not category A but are under category A conditions and that's morally indefensible too, because many don't need to be there and the cost is phenomenal. There's probably a good case for reducing high security estates; that would save money, and I do strongly believe in finding areas to save.

Sarah

I don't think prison will ever work. If it hasn't made a difference now, I don't think it ever will. It's just a way of life for some, it doesn't matter how much incarceration they do, they'll never change. I nipped into town this morning and saw two lads. It was, alright Miss, how you doing? I've just got out. I bump into loads of ex-prisoners. I see lads begging and take them to Greggs for a sandwich and a cup of tea instead of giving them money for drugs. I'm on sick with stress, and I do miss the job but I can't go back. My daughter begged me not to go into work, because I'd come home after a thirteen hour shift and be physically exhausted and mentally drained. You get five or six incidents every day now. Assaults on staff are worse. Assaults on prisoners are worse. Drugs are worse.

Peter

Prisons and Probation are much better at public protection than rehabilitation. Some might argue, that's fine, that's the way it should be, but there are a range of reasons for that, that the Probation Service is neither equipped nor required to address. I can't address housing policy, I can't address unemployment, the level of benefit. I can't produce adequate mental health resources. There are no simple answers, but the answers there are, are interlinked, across a range of things. I do think multi-agency stuff is the way forward, but it's resource intensive so it's unpopular. There have been nights as a younger man where, if I'd turned right instead of left, the whole script could have been different, and I don't forget that. I learned something very valuable from a nurse once, which I've applied throughout my career She said, when I meet somebody, I try not to focus on whether or not I like them, or whether or not I approve or disapprove, but what service I would want this person to have if they were a member of my family. And that gets me through tough times because I meet some thoroughly dislikeable people. Most of the people I've met, you wouldn't approve of the things they've done or the choices they've made.

John

In the early days you got to know prisoners, you had time. I enjoyed going to work because I had a class of twelve people I was doing an induction course with, or a drugs course. You'd go in the next day and they'd done bits of homework. They made huge life-lines from when they were born, fabulous artistic stuff, right through to the day they came into prison, and because you were doing a course with them for a week, a fortnight, a month, they put effort in for you. It started to change about 2010. I loved going in and having a crack, and you knew they were blagging you, they'd be nice to your face and call you worse than shit in the cell, but it was an interaction and it was good. Now, you might see them for five minutes in a morning and five minutes on a night. There's no bond. I look out onto the empty wing and think, what the hell am I doing here? I'm better than this. I'm better than just walking from one end of the wing to the other, opening all the doors, saying cheerio and then sitting in the office eating doughnuts and drinking coffee 'til they come back.

Donna

Open prisons prepare people for release. You go out on placements, get into the habit of shopping and looking after yourself. But there's hardly any of them. Apart from that, all prison does is totally institutionalise. Everything is taken away from you. You're left with nothing and then you're chucked out and told right, now you have to be a totally functioning human being, you have to fend for yourself and think again. We need far more open prisons and open houses. I'd have just a few prisons, for those that really need to be imprisoned, and the clinically insane should be in psychiatric units. There is a certain amount of people that should be in prison, of course there is, but only a few compared to the amount now. I've been told by a good friend, a manager at a probation hostel, that because of the cutbacks, they can't even buy a bottle of milk out of petty cash. They're not allowed to give bus fares, so lads on licence might miss reporting to the police, or reporting to the courts, then get recalled. They can't give them anything, so they may as well be in prison. A hostel used to be about rehabilitation and now that feels punitive as well. It's as if all the kindness and respect has gone, to be replaced by punitive measures. And life's not that black and white is it? The thing with prisons is, you'd go in, you'd have this hour and a half with someone you knew, you'd motivate them, say, this is what we're going to do, there is light beyond the tunnel, and if you behave you can have this and do that. But then they brought the cutbacks, and they don't get the support anymore, and somebody's working them to death, and there's a prison officer saying he'll do something and he doesn't. And all our plans are cut back, so we don't get a chance to see him anymore. Imagine you're going on a long journey, and halfway through that journey, you have everything taken away from you. How do you carry on? Where's your motivation? That's what happens to lads in prison.

Stephen

I get worried when people focus on difference rather than the basic core humanity and sameness we all have. Respect and explore differences, but if we focus on othering people, history shows us it's always easier to do bad things.

Peter

The climate to do things for people has moved. Successive governments have been tough on crime, stating we're tougher than they were. We're not going to call it community service anymore, or reparation, repairing the harm done to communities, because that smacks of positivity. We're going to call it unpaid work or community punishment. They're still doing up old folks gardens and council estates, but let's call it something different and make them wear high vis jackets. Bollocks. You get guys who've completed community service before, and now they're saying, I'm not doing unpaid fucking work. Why not have some positive association with it? Why not say you've been of service to the community? Mrs Whatever down the street has got her garden done because you've done that. And let's be fair, the organisational priorities have changed, the resources with which to deliver those priorities have changed, and we're very much not social workers, we're risk managers and we expect them to take responsibility for their offending. I just don't think that's completely realistic, people are offending for complex reasons.

Adele

I've heard prisoners say, prison's not that bad, I get my pad and my telly, a bit of pocket money and association, it gives me a break from being on the streets and somewhere to dry out. These are short term prisoners. The longer ones are doing a longer time, but it's the short term prisoners that are more likely to re-offend. It was the same when I worked with lifer women. They were doing the bulk of the time but they were the least likely to re-offend. Short term sentences just don't work. Prison should be tougher and harder for them. You know what's going to stop a lot of lads going back in there? When the no smoking ban comes in. Make it hard for them. I'd take away every damn thing. Some of them have the life of Riley to what they've had outside. It would be horrendous if you've got a settled home life, but for half of these it's better than what they've ever had. They've got their own bed, somewhere to put their clothes, they know where their next meal is coming from. I'd ban smoking and the gym. I know the gym can be a stress buster, but why should they be able to come into prison and beef up? If they're conforming and you can see signs of remorse, then fine, but to have gym four or five times a week? And they complain about going to a class with ten or twelve students. I'd have loved that for my kids. I only get £1.50 a day for coming to this shit. Well, if you were out there mate, you'd be paying for it. Whatever we're doing is not working, is it? Because they keep coming back again. It's really sad, working all these years and saying that. It's keeping them off the streets and maybe keeping society a bit safer for a while, and I know we've got to do something with them so we might as well try, but even the lads know they're on an easy number. And when you see what they've been brought up with, there's no guidance. They haven't had parents insisting they go to school, or they've played the class clown and been on drugs since they were eleven. They haven't had a chance from the beginning.

Donna

Prison doesn't work. For some people yes, keep them locked away because they're a risk to the public, but they're few and far between. Prison just causes more damage. They become institutionalised. Drugs, everything. You have a record, come out and nobody wants to know you, it just doesn't work.

What would work?

A more caring society. More jobs. A decent benefit amount. Not having to turn to drugs if you have mental health issues. Daily support for people who need it. But if someone commits an offence and you just bang them up, when they come back out, if someone's off their head, or they've no money for electricity, or to eat, then you have to spend your time sorting all that out, rather than saying, oh, can you just sit there while I do a cognitive behaviour programme on your anger management. It's that chaotic lifestyle again. They put all the money into prisons to just bang somebody up, but hardly any to work with them before or after, it's mad.

Keith

If Prison and Probation could work well together, we could actually begin to reduce re-offending, do real rehabilitation and get prisoners back to positive lives. When you talk to offenders, the vast majority just want somewhere to live, a job, and a relationship with someone where they can settle down and live a normal life. But when you see the experiences they've had prior to prison, it's not surprising that's where they end up. And with this current political set up we've got, I don't have any real hope of achieving real progress.

Alice

Education has changed completely in the twelve years I've taught. There's hardly any classes like the ones I teach, they're more geared to where funding comes from, so English and Maths, Literacy and

Numeracy, Basic Skills, and they are important but it shouldn't be to the detriment of all other subjects. This need some of the men have for opening up facets of their own personal lives; it's really important. Some prisoners have committed horrific crimes, especially sexual offenders, and have minds that have become perverted and twisted in many ways. Now I'm not a psychologist, but I've always had an interest in it, and I did do Post Graduate Studies with Philosophy and Psychology, and that twist, when it's unravelled, there can be something positive there, when you get it involved in creative stuff. There might be some eccentric personalities which, if given a different environment to the one they've grown up in, may never have committed a crime. There's a reverse side to every coin. Whatever is very good in someone has the potential to be very bad, and vice versa. And I really do think the prison system needs to open its mind because they're missing a golden opportunity to rehabilitate, to get people back into society where they can actually contribute.

Peter

Most people have a genuine desire not to go to jail, until they've a peer group inside. Then it becomes an acceptable occupational hazard, and in some ways, for some people, career advancement, because you make alliances, people can see your backbone, and they can see whether your tongue's loose. But there'd be an awful lot more people committing crime if they weren't expecting a consequence like deprivation of liberty, and some people have done such damaging things, especially offences against the person, that they need to be locked up, as well as we need them to be locked up. You and I wouldn't want to live in a society where they didn't have prisons because we'd be eaten alive.

Adele

Mental health is a big thing, but a lot is wrongly blamed on mental health. Their brains are pickled with drugs. I'll never forget this guy. I said, you're out in three months, what's your plan? He said, I've

worked two years as a brickie, I've done my bit, I'm putting my feet up.
I said, you're twenty-eight. I don't need too much, he said, I've got my
flat, a fridge, a few cans, a chair and a telly. But you're twenty-eight.
I know, I'm putting my feet up, I'm done. Anyway, I've got mental
health problems. You're as fit as a butcher's dog, I said. I get anxiety,
he said, I can't cope. How can you give somebody a working culture
when they're not interested? There's some big companies around here
that run initiatives to get people into work, but if they don't want to do
it in the first place, it's not going to happen is it? And I do think he's
representative of many of the lads I see. They go to the gym three or
four times a week, but they've got mental health issues? If they can
do that, they must be able to do some job in a factory. You hear them.
Listen mate, when you go to the doctors, this is what you need to say.
They're playing the system and us taxpayers are paying for them. Too
many of them know how to do it, they just go through their whole life
getting what they can for nothing, and what they can't get for nothing
they'll rob, so they can get their drugs or whatever. It's a vicious circle.
Some go out and get themselves settled, of course they do, but not
most of them. Eighty percent say, I'm going back out there and I'm going on the sick. That's what they do. That's their goal.

Caroline

There's a massive blaming culture where perpetrators blame victims or circumstances, or their pasts. The majority might admit what
they've done but it's backed up with an excuse, so they don't take responsibility for their actions. That's where one-to-one works much
better, as in, right, you admit you've done this, let's look at the reasons
behind it. And if you look at patterns of past behaviour, the offences
and patterns afterwards, you often can break it down with people. And
fundamentally, you have to believe that people can change. If you don't
have some level of belief that people can change and address their be-
haviours, then you can't do the job with any conviction. And people
can change, but they need support and guidance because they often get
entrenched in their behaviour and their environment and can't see a
way out. I worked with lots of eighteen, nineteen year olds in the field

team and they used to drive me round the bend. But I've seen quite a few of them subsequently, a few years down the line, and they come up and say, guess what, I've got a family and a job. And I like to think I might have played a part in that.

Alice

My job was like a ministry to me. I remember a priest once told me that, and I was taken aback but it struck a chord and it's true. I can't separate what I'm teaching from the whole notion of personhood and dignity and respect, conveying something that can actually change the world a little bit for whoever is receiving it. It gives them a stronger sense of who they are, through the knowledge they acquire. And knowledge does change you.

Peter

When we joined, we hoped to be that one with the magic word, that reached across the table and got the rapport, and someone said, yes, I've seen the fucking light, thank you so much. But actually what we're doing is planting seeds. The way to get people to change behaviour is not by moral or rational argument, it's by identifying self-interest for them. And part of the reason we're sat in this room is the moral argument has been lost already. There's almost no point telling people it's wrong to steal things. Someone in kindergarten told them that and they were not fucking convinced. What I've got to do is convince you that your life would work better if you're not doing this shit. We plant seeds. If the guy I'm with is twenty-eight years old, and he's going to stop burgling when he's forty, but I can work with him to help him stop when he's thirty-three, that seems a realistic aspiration. I aint found the magic word. If I had, I'd have wrapped it and sold it to the Home Office a long time ago, and I'd be teaching people all over the world.

Stephen

It's always going to be a world of challenge. It's never going to be a world where we've done it, that's a fantasy. But we can create a world where prisons are much more effectively manned and where we help people with their lives in such a way that there's a much lower chance of them going back into prison.

A Handful Of Pebbles

Antonio

My only source of reference now, to my children and my wife, after a decade and a quarter, the only anecdotes, the only stories I can tell that are pertinent to conversations going on, are ones that happened in prison. I feel like fucking Red off Shawshank Redemption sometimes. That time of my life was fucking traumatic for everyone concerned, so if I'm telling a funny story about prison, that misses the fact that there was millions of minutes of insane boredom, and anguish about being ripped away from my family, and relentless month after month and year after year. The anecdotes are funny, but they're like a sandy beach and somebody's threw a handful of pebbles. All the sand is the minutes you've been in prison and the pebbles are the funny stories I'm telling my kids. And the kids think, oh you had a great time in prison, cooking fucking lasagne, but they don't realise that all those thousands of millions of grains of sand were really what it was like. It gives them a false sense of perception.

Colin

You get lots of self-centred people in prison. I guess some of that is nature, but a lot's through necessity. You have to look after number one in prison. It teaches you to be more self-serving and less humane to others. You can't afford to be soft on people, or other people will walk all over you and you'll be seen as a target.

Rebecca

People always said, why don't you move out the estate? But I think about the lady from the 7-11 bombing. She was living in Israel, she came here to avoid being bombed and she got bombed in Britain, so whatever's meant to happen, it will happen regardless. And sometimes situations happen and it's not about you, it's about people around you, for you to have some input. But if my dad didn't pass away early, things might have been different, because my boys didn't have a father figure, even though I was their mum and they respected me. When my dad died, that was the time Errol and Nathan started getting into trouble. They looked up to him and would have been able to talk to him about certain situations. He'd have taken them places, they'd have seen different things. I don't know. I used to think that if I'd stayed in Trinidad, then I wouldn't have a bad life, because I was living with my dad's father and that lady that brought me up.

Sophie

I don't ever remember seeing my dad get arrested. I don't even know all the things he was arrested for and I don't want to know. And clearly prison hasn't stopped him committing crime as he's always going back in there. I personally think he might enjoy it in prison, because why else would you keep doing things to go back?

Val

I'm past that aggressive stage now. I've got a man who would never hit me. I've got my kids where I want them to be, well not the oldest one, I dragged her out a crack-house the other day and chucked her in the back of the car. But I've been out a couple of years and sometimes I wish I was back there. Things are hard. I've got one daughter who's on drugs and takes all my money off me. I've got an autistic daughter who needs attention all the time and is constantly waking me up. And when I argue with them, which I always do, because I won't let anyone walk all over me, I think, this is too hard out here, I can't do it. And I long sometimes to go back, to see the screws that were kind. One of them used to tuck me up in bed every night.

Colin

Through a small copse of trees, as the sunlight ripples and shifts on surrounding mountains, and our destination finally appears in front. Colin jumps out the car, grabs his camera and walks to giant rocks, planted thousands of years earlier and precisely placed in a circle to celebrate the winter solstice. Smooth grooved and angular, wind-shaved cracked, mottled in green and yellow lichen and prickled in quartz. He puts his hand on the first stone. Foxgloves sprout from its base, rising up from modern life offerings of shiny beads and plastic trinkets. And then he moves his hand over the surface of the stone and looks up at the screech of an unknown bird.

When I get opportunities to come out into the countryside, I seize them, because you don't know what tomorrow's going to bring. I go out every day, to stop myself finding an excuse to stay in. I've got a lot of time to make up, and I feel like I'm living on a knife edge with Probation, I feel under threat every day. There's no risk of me going back to prison after this licence finishes, none at all. But I'm thinking of moving abroad, because you always have a past in this country. If I go somewhere else, I can have a future. And I just want to be free and live in peace. Whatever struggles and challenges come along, they won't really matter after this constant threat of going back to prison. It makes you ill. I'm worried for my own physical and mental health all the time. I'm being treated for my mental health at the moment, for stress and anxiety and depression. I didn't worry about that when I was on the inside, you're left alone most the time, it's now I'm out. That's why we're having serious conversations about me going back to prison. My girlfriend sees the pressure I'm put under by Probation, or rather that particular officer. And it wouldn't make sense to me, unless I'd lived through it, to think I wasn't stressed and feeling ill in prison, but I am now I've been released. It wouldn't make any sense why people would choose to go back to prison, because it makes it sound as if prison is a soft option and it's not. I've seen people seriously hurt. I've seen people stabbed. People have been killed in horrendous ways. Prisons make people bitter, that's the only things they do. They take people away from the community, but they don't do anything with them apart from negative things. And I have met some truly evil people, and society needs protecting from them, but I don't know if they have mental health problems, or if society or prison has helped shape them to what they are now. It stamps out humanity, prison, it stamps it out of your soul. If you're too humane you won't survive it. It makes hard men harder. You have little pity for others because you can't afford it. I think that's what I meant about learning to be selfish. Rehabilitation doesn't exist, not at all. And I don't know what shape it could take in this country, because it has to be with the will of the public doesn't it? The media, with the public, decide on what sort of prison system we have, and I don't know what system the public would stomach. I think the media has an enormous amount of blood on its hands, when it comes to the penal systems and crime, because it makes the system what it is. We've all seen these stories about prisoners having it soft, with their meals and game machines, with this, that and the other. People probably believe it and think prisons should get tougher, but I've never known any prisoner living it up in prison. And if they do have a games machine they've earned it through enhanced privileges and they've had to buy it, and they're not new, they're ancient machines. And if they eat well, they're buying it themselves, or doing what I did and extorting other prisoners, or selling drugs. Justice has to be seen to be done of course, but I don't think locking people up and forgetting about them is the way to do it, which is why I agree with the death penalty. It's more humane to put people to death than to give them a life sentence without any hope.

Paige

Still scratching her wrist, though softer now, Paige has been smiling more freely for the last half hour of our chat.

Before, I couldn't give a damn, I'd just go and twat someone, but now I think about the consequences. I've got two kids and a house and I've settled down. I don't drink, I prefer a takeaway and a DVD. And I want to make something of my life. But it's tough. The kids know what buttons to press. I had an emotional breakdown so I'm on sedating tablets and everything, but life still goes on.

I say my thank you's and leave. I drive the wrong way, turn around and come back past her house again, just thirty seconds later. She's crossing the street before me, a mobile phone pushed onto her ear and a frown on her face. I wave. She puts her hand up in acknowledgement and then she's behind me, and I'm driving out of her estate, towards new green leaves and spring blossom.

Daniel

Past a football ground, past cranes that point up to the heavens. Sunshine fights through grey and reflects from the sides of buildings acting like giant mirrors, highlighting a daddy swinging his little boy to squeals of delight. We pass Turkish, Indian and Chinese restaurants, Mongolian and Greek restaurants, then head outwards on a dual carriageway. Daniel tells me he has no idea where he is. I take my mobile phone from my pocket to find out; two hours of driving and we're only ten minutes away from our start. Just take the next left I say, and turn right at the top.

Up until me going to high security, I didn't want to change my life. But sitting in high security, talking to other prisoners that wished they was me, with a release date, with a good family, I realised it wasn't worth it, because if I'd got out of prison and carried on doing what I was doing, I would have ended up as one of these people that never had a release date. And I couldn't think of anything worse, to think I'm never getting out. That's what did it for me. But I honestly believe that a prisoner will never change his ways, no matter how many times you sit and talk to him, no matter how many fucking courses you put him on, or her on, unless they want to, unless they're ready to. So sitting there, drilling into them that it's bad to do this, it's bad to do that, they're not bothered. But if you got a prisoner doing twelve months and took him out of the local or C Cat and whacked him in high security for five or six weeks, with people that were never going home, and let him sit there with these people, doing normal things like going to the gym and having dinner with them, and listening to them about what they're saying, about their appeals and how they're never going to see their kids, how they're not allowed to give their daughter away at a wedding and things like that, I think that would be the thing that would change a lot of people. Because I never thought I'd stop what I was doing, never, and I have. I don't do anything now. I go to work Monday to Friday, every single week. I work my bollocks off. I have my own little company and I've done all that in a year. I've got a brand new company car, I've got a nice house, a nice family, and it's all because I wanted that to happen. I can remember talking to this prisoner in high security, and he was known as the most successful drug dealer in the country, and I said to him, how long have you got left? And he said, nineteen years, but I'm not bothered because I've got two million to get out to. And I thought to myself, if he's the most successful drug dealer in this country, then fuck that, it aint worth it. It's like people who burgle houses. What are you gonna nick from there, a telly? A couple of gold rings and two grand cash? You're getting four or five years for that, it's not worth it anymore. It never was worth it to begin with, but now I've finally realised.

Gary

It hits me the most at Christmas. I cry every time. But we look forward to the future now. There's light at the end of the tunnel, just one more birthday and one more Christmas inside, then seven more months and he's out. And he's got himself a girlfriend, a girl he met ages ago, his best mate's sister. She's always loved him she said. She's two years older with two lovely kids, her own place, and she's lovely too. She goes and sees him. I took her last Friday.

Craig

Craig stops and looks down at his feet. A blue tit, he says. Look at the size of it, it must have just come out the nest. He bends down. I hope you learn soon son, because a cat will pick you up. Go on, back you go. He tries to waft it back into the long grass. It tweets and shuf-fles onto a nettle leaf, so he picks it up and puts it in the long grass himself. If it's out here like that, he says, showing no fear, a dog or a cat will snap it straight up, or kids will kick it. And then we continue walking along the side of the lake.

It's weird, looking back now, because it was such a big part of me life. Every now and then, you're sat in the living room, you'll go into the kitchen and think, inside I couldn't even do this. Or if I'm coming back from the shops and it's half six I'll think God, I'd be locked up half an hour now and I wouldn't be out until tomorrow morning. You think it's going to take over, but when the rest of your life starts getting mixed back in, it does start blending into the background a bit. It's taken a while and it's always going to be there, but I'm glad about that because it does make you think twice about everything you do. People who say it's an easy life, believe us it's not, they're kidding themselves. And the media talks shite, absolute shite, because what they forget is, yes you might have a television, or you might even have a computer game, but your punishment is the loss of liberty. You can't see your family, you can't do nothing. Even if you ring your family, you can only ring them when they say you can ring them, and you know your call is getting recorded so you can't be yourself. To me, that's the punish-ment, not what you lose materially. Even the televisions and smoking and stuff like that, that's not a treat for prisoners, it's a control mecha-nism by staff, because they said once they put TV's in, violence quar-tered. Smoking relieves peoples tension, stops them getting all worked up. They're not doing things like that for the sake of prisoners, they're doing it for their own sakes.

Rebecca

Rebecca's younger sister Jane arrives, followed by her son Na-than, all broad shouldered and muscular, with a big grin and a gold tooth. Nathan tells me his Aunty Jane bullies him and Jane laughs. She says she's looking out for him, making sure he stays on the right path. Rebecca looks upon her son, her eyes full of love and admira-

tion mixed with worry. *I stand up to leave and get a warm hand-shake from Nathan, before Rebecca opens her arms and we hug.*

We went to church every Sunday. My children didn't watch nothing violent on TV because I was strict in the home. It was school during the week, then bible studies, youth club or prayer meetings, then Saturday at home and church on Sunday, and from there you might go to one of the other families and have dinner together. So when Nathan got in this trouble, I prayed, God was my refuge. And people might not understand, but I know God. All the things I've been through, God has been there for me. He told me when Nathan got sentenced, if Daniel didn't go into the lion's den, then he wouldn't have shut the mouth of the lion. Nathan is a general in God's army, that's the word I get. Errol, all that God will say to me is, you don't need to worry, he belongs to me. Nathan I did worry about, but I knew he wasn't going to come out the same. And I know God's got a plan, and some of it's going to be hard, but that's God's plan and purpose. Because when Nathan got that sentence, that's what broke me, and I was saying, God, I trusted in you, I believed in you. I watched a Christian video where there was a Chinese man in prison, and he didn't have no legs, he was fasting and praying, and you know in China they don't have no time when they're coming out. But the lord opened the door, and the man walked out, and I believe the lord was telling me, that's what I'm going to do, I'm going to bring Nathan out when I'm ready. And a lot of people say Nathan's lost fifteen years of his life, but he hasn't, he's gained fifteen years.

Sophie

Before my dad went back to prison, all he ever used to talk about was my little sister, which was nice for her but not for me. He tried to contact me once and I asked him to arrange a visit. That was six months ago and I still haven't heard a word. So that's closure for me, I don't want anything else to do with him.

Val

Down through muddy woods we walk, Val placing her feet extra carefully so she doesn't slip on her back once again, her little dog panting from chasing so many pheasants. Then we're on flat ground and walking back towards my car in the village. Val grasps sticks and feathers she's gathered from our walk, and in the other hand she has a clump of elderberries she's chewing on.

I'm working with this organisation now. They're the shits of an organisation, they're not bothered about people, they're bothered about numbers. I help people with addiction and serious offences, people who've come out of prison, the mentally ill, domestic violence, carers, everything. I work in the gym, but if they've just come out of prison and they've been chucked on the streets, I ring round and find them somewhere. I put one of the lads up myself. If they've got no food I'll sort them a food parcel. If someone had said to me I'd end up in jail and be working with people on drugs, I'd say, fuck that. I used to tell them, get off your fucking arses and get a job like me. But now I know it's an illness, and I remember, when I got beat up so badly, these two crack-heads picked me up and took me to this house. You had to climb in through the top window. They got me some fags and a couple of cans and looked after me, and they never had money of their own. I was full of sovereigns all over my body, I stayed there two days and they bathed my cuts while the helicopters were out looking. So now I look after people with drug problems, even though I hated them two years ago when I was inside. But with all the experiences I've been through, I couldn't be working in a better place. And I know that when death comes to them places, which is regular, I can say to them, fucking snap yourself out of it, because the next person going through that door could be you.

Billy

Their baby is whinging and starting to cry. Billy's girlfriend brings her over and apologises for the noise. Don't worry, I say, it's fine. She holds the baby out towards Billy, who takes her and sits her on his knee. He kisses the baby's cheek and makes silly noises and their baby begins to laugh instead.

I don't think I'll ever go back to prison. I've got family now. There's a lot more to life. I've met a lot of people who are still in prison, or who are still going back. I didn't have much to live for when I was young, and I didn't care. I've got a head on my shoulders now. A lot of my friends are obsessed about being gangsters or the local hard man. I was just stupid or violent and I've grown up. I've got my Mrs and my baby daughter. I didn't know what life was about. I never even knew what love was until I met my girlfriend, but I know now.

Gary

Jack's always said, I'm glad I went to prison dad, because I was on the drugs before. And I never even knew because we hadn't been that close for years, and he blamed me for his parents splitting up. I knew he'd tried to kill himself, I was standing in the back garden having a tab one night when the police helicopter came over. I never realised it was for my own son until the police pulled up in a car. And that's why I blame myself, because he couldn't even tell his own dad what was wrong. He used to text me and tell me to fuck off on Father's Day. But the relationship we have now is unbelievable. He's sent me a stack of letters and now he makes me things for Father's Day. Life's a strange thing.

Antonio

Into their house we go, tastefully decorated by Layla. She tells me she worked fourteen hour shifts six days a week to get enough money to visit Antonio in prison. She puts the kettle on and points at a huge print of Bob Marley on the wall, then tells me she painted it, and his quote underneath, before allowing me time to read it. 'Who are you to judge the life I live? I am not perfect and I don't have to be. Before you start pointing fingers, make sure your own hands are clean.' And then Antonio sits on his couch and rolls another cannabis joint.

I went to jail when I was younger and I had, well, the word is an epiphany. I started looking at why I'd got into all this shite and why I'd been so fucked up all my life. I mean, I actually thought I was crazy, I must be because I'd done some really crazy things and they seemed logical at the time. I was sat in a cell with tears in my eyes, and a screw was going to get his mates because I'd been physical with him and smashed my cell to pieces. And I was looking at myself thinking, I didn't get up this morning to plan this, why is my life like this? And I realised I had no control over my life. So I looked into psychology, I went down the library and got every book on it, and obviously I had every single symptom in every single book, it was a ridiculous thing to do. So I became knowledgeable about psychology over the centuries but not knowledgeable about myself. And then I got into meditation. There was one single golden thread through every psychological book I read, which said every client got benefits from meditation, and of course I'm in a cell twenty three hours a day, you can't get a better fucking place to meditate. But the library was so old and shit that the book I got was from the 1930's and was the most tiresome and arduous form of meditation you could possibly do. I didn't know any other though, so I just cracked on. I did it twenty minutes a day when the jail went to sleep over dinner and fucking hell, I had some astonishing moments over the next two and a half years, just astonishing, and I was stone cold sober. Most of the time it's trying to get your thoughts under control, in order, and now and again you reach a state where there is calm and you can see the universe, I can't describe it better than that. You can feel every thought and hear every word. You can feel every planet. You know this physical experience you're going through is mystical and ageless. Unfortunately, when you're opened up on the wing and you're emptying a piss bucket, you soon lose those fucking illusions, but they do remain deep in your core. I became master of my own thoughts, master of my own feelings and desires. I decided when I was going to get angry, when I needed to be determined and when I needed to get emotional. Basically, I had control of myself. And I was able to find out my goals in life, and my goals at that age, as a young guy from the orphanage and the ghetto, were to make sure my family would never ever be fucking born as orphans ever again, and to get my kids and their kids as far away from the streets and being fucking dumped in boxes by forlorn prostitutes as possible. And so I became materialistic and I used that awakening, that spiritual power and energy, in the right way originally, but then I got past financial security and I started getting into ridiculousness, and once I got greedy that's when I needed a slap on the arse and that decade in jail. And that's got me back into my true ambition, which is more altruistic, and more than just saving my own kids, it's saving as many orphans who are sitting in boxes right here today, while I'm breathing. But I've got my own five kids to save first, because they've been missing their dad for almost thirteen years.

The Cast

Craig has one year left on licence and has been signed onto the Sex Offenders Register for life. He is currently studying for qualifications in Warehousing and Power Machinery.

Val has finished on licence and gone travelling around the Far East.

Daniel is on licence for another seven years. Still working, he has ambitious plans to expand his truck driving business.

Colin has three years left on licence. His Probation Officer still refuses to allow him to work.

Antonio was recalled to prison for three months, because he was living at his wife's home, rather than the house that was allocated as his approved premises. He has since been released and has ten years left on licence.

Billy is working in a gym six days a week, in order to look after his young family.

Paige continues to look after her two young children.

Peter is still working at Crown Court, writing sentencing reports.

Donna has retired from the Probation Service on medical grounds.

Caroline continues working alongside Probation and Community Rehabilitation Companies, employed by a national charity.

John has retired from the Prison Service and has a 'no stress' part-time job.

Sarah has finished her sickness leave and resigned from the privatised prison.

Keith continues to work in the field of Criminal Justice, in the areas of consultancy and research.

Stephen continues to work in Psychology, and continues to specalise in prisons.

Adele is still teaching men in a local prison but is hoping to resurrect her dream of running a massage and acupuncture business.

Alice has stopped working in prisons and now teaches private one-to-one sessions.

Nigel has moved abroad for three years but plans to come back into prison education on his return.

Rebecca still has two sons and one brother in prison.

Gary is praying his son will be released on licence in 2018.

Sophie is trying to progress in life and forget about her father.

Acknowledgements

Richard would like to thank the following:

All of my interviewees, for their time, company and honesty. I have not used their real names, in order to obscure their identity

Andrew Lownie, for his excellent advice

Gillian Peace, for her proof-reading skills

Professor Maggie O'Neill, for her support and foreword

Erwin James, for reading and loving the manuscript

My wife Anna, for putting up with me, and so much more

thetruthaboutprison.com welcomes your views and thoughts about this book and our criminal justice system. Feel free to give your view or join a debate under the relevant posts: Prisoners, Professionals and Families. You can also e-mail richard@lapwingbooks.com.

Lapwing Books is on Facebook. Richard W Hardwick is on Facebook and Twitter. Feel free to connect.

The Truth About Prison is available on Kindle and other devices.

Universities and other organisations can purchase discounted copies of this book if buying in bulk. Please e-mail richard@lapwingbooks. com for further information.

Receive the heart-rending short story 'Rooftops' for free when you sign up to Lapwing Books mailing list at lapwingbooks.com

Andalucía by Richard W Hardwick

Told with courage, humour and love, *Andalucía* weaves past and present with great skill so the pace of the narrative never falters. A zest for life on every page that I found both moving and inspiring

Pat Barker, winner of The Booker Prize

This absolutely captivated me. I couldn't put it down. One of the best books I've read ... breath-taking

Janette Jenkins – author of Angel of Brooklyn, Little Bones and Firefly

Kicked Out by Richard W Hardwick

A novel to stand up alongside Irvine Welsh's Trainspotting, offering a window into the youth of today. A fantastic book expressing the cynicism and dissatisfaction of those on the edge of society

Waterstone's Recommended Read

The narrative is so strong, the characters and dialogue so real, the situation so heart-breaking. This is masterful and should win several literary prizes

Patricia J. Delois, award-winning author of *Bufflehead Sisters*

Hardwick's writing has the power and humanity to make you wonder about the way you see the world, and to give voice to those whose stories usually remain untold

Laura Brewis, New Writing North